No More Running in Circles

by

Kim Engelmann

&

Teresa McBean

Cover art by Rachel Hartshorn of Hartshorn Books

ISBN-13: 978-1494486358
ISBN-10: 1494486350

Printed in the United States of America

Table of Contents

Prologue

Teresa McBean

In early 2008, someone sent me a copy of Kim's book, *Running In Circles*. I stayed up all night and read it (the first time) in one sitting. I used my limited ability to navigate the World Wide Web, found her email address (a miracle), and sent her an email. I don't normally behave like an Internet stalker, but I simply had to tell Kim that her book touched my heart in ways that were too sacred to ignore. I thanked her for writing about her suffering while treating with respect those who had caused her harm. I expressed appreciation for the finesse and grace it must have taken to write about her suffering without sounding like she was a victim. She managed to convince me, the reader, that she told the truth without sugarcoating or shaming others. I figured she must be a woman of integrity. I never expected to hear from her, but she graciously wrote me back, and we've since found ways to connect. I consider it a grand privilege to call her my friend. I want you to know that you can trust the work she will ask you to do, because she herself has walked this same path. Kim is the real deal, and she is showing us how we can become "real" too. (Remember *The Velveteen Rabbit*? That kind of real…)

We can learn how to tell the truth, experience transformation, and heal from the inevitable wounds that come from living on planet earth. Kim and I believe that sometimes it is helpful to have some structure to help with this process, so we have collaborated. She tells her story, gives us a marvelous metaphor of hamster-wheel versus potter's-wheel suffering to explain the process, and provides a workbook to assist us in applying this powerful picture to our own experiences. The structure Kim has chosen to use is the 12-step model. I've jumped in and inserted myself into her lovely body of work with some additional conversation around the 12-step process. We hope you find this approach helpful!

This book, along with the accompanying workbook, provides participants the opportunity to re-evaluate previously held notions about what it means to believe that there is a God. We're telling Kim's personal story, using her excellent metaphors of hamster-wheel versus potter's-wheel suffering, and giving an overview of the 12 steps from a Christian perspective. We pray that these various ways of talking about faith and suffering will provide you tools to process your own pain and experience God in a new way. We believe these materials present a process that is both comforting and challenging, much like the message Kim received sitting on her couch all those years ago.

Before we begin, I want to introduce you to the concept of the 12 steps, assuming you don't already know them. The 12 steps are a remarkable spiritual tool which many users speak about as "life transforming." I know some folks think they are only for people with addiction issues. As a pastor working within the context of a recovery ministry and as Executive Director of the National Association for Christian Recovery, my experience has taught me that these steps have transformative potential for anyone willing to work them—not just addicts and their beloved co-dependents.

All of us—every single person I've ever known—desperately needs transformation. Some of us are aware of our need for change, and some are not. Some of us become willing to admit our need for rescue. Sadly, some remain stubbornly resistant. All of us, whether we acknowledge it or not, struggle with living out God's promise to restore and his exhortation to embrace the work of faithful living (See James 1 and Romans 12). If we think for just a few seconds about the scripture's descriptions of faithful living in contrast to our own personal experiences with selfishness, abuse, neglect and cruelty, it's not a stretch for us to admit that we need help learning how to live faithfully. I myself know it's difficult to find examples of faithfulness to follow. Yet I dare to dream that if I work these steps, I might learn a new way to live…and perhaps have an experience I can share with others in need of a path out of bondage and into the light of recovery. Here's one biblical description of the problem we face:

> "There's nobody living right, not even one, nobody who knows the score, nobody alert for God. They've all taken the wrong turn; they've all wandered down blind alleys. No one's living right; I can't find a single one. Their throats are gaping graves, their tongues slick as mud slides. Every word they speak is tinged with poison. They open their mouths and pollute the air. They race for the honor of sinner-of-the-year, litter the land with heartbreak and ruin, don't know the first thing about living with others. They never give God the time of day. This makes it clear, doesn't it, that whatever is written in these Scriptures is not what God says about others but to us to whom these Scriptures were addressed in the first place! And it's clear enough, isn't it, that we're sinners, every one of us, in the same sinking boat with everybody else?" (Romans 3:10-20 The Message)

Our need for transformation is real; but I say frankly (as Kim also does throughout this book), it's the end game. Transformation isn't achieved through self-help, self-control, or even a sincere wishing to "be ye transformed" as the King James Version of scripture says. It is the great gift of addiction that has taught us this. Addicts know what the rest of us need to learn: our lives are unmanageable, we need a power greater than ourselves to restore us to sanity, and this power, our God, is respectful of us. We must surrender and turn our lives over to his care and control in order to turn him loose to do his part in the transforming process.

I don't want to spoil the book for you, but here's the thing: if you work these steps using Kim's workbook, absorb Kim's story, and try to understand its implications for your own life, I predict that you will discover that God has WAY more to do with your experience of transformation than you ever will. This is good news. But you also have a part, and Kim is going to guide us through this with authenticity, wisdom, and kindness. Hear her story by reading this book, consider using the companion study guide to help guide you through the process, and ask God to show up on your behalf…and let's see what happens.

May your time with her prove as life changing for you as it did for me and my friends!

Teresa McBean, Executive Director
National Association for Christian Recovery

Chapter 1

Trapped in a Cycle of Pain

Kim Engelmann

"And you call yourself a Christian!"

I noticed how tight and white my mother's lips were when she spoke. She was standing on the stair landing above me, hands on her hips.

"You'll never get into heaven with an attitude like that! God knows all the evil thoughts you've ever had about me. Not one is hidden from him."

She continued down the steps, her index finger pointed at me. Her footsteps were heavy; the stubby heels of her black shoes thudding. The thin pale lips were moving again.

"You'll never please God the way you are. Don't think you won't reap the consequences of your evil thoughts. 'Vengeance is mine. I will repay, says the Lord!'" She was upon me now.

I was eleven. I had vacuumed the house and, according to my mother, not done a very good job. I was not fond of vacuuming, and when she ordered me to do it over, I had pushed back. I thought I had done a great job, and besides, it was a daunting task. Our house was a historic faculty home on the campus of a well-endowed institution for higher learning. There were fireplaces in every room, and the rooms were immense.

Maybe she was angry because I had spent time with my father that morning listening to his lecture. He had read it to me with his glasses balanced on the end of his nose. She didn't like it when Dad and I spent time alone. But I wasn't really sure what had set off this episode. I never was.

"If you knew the truth - that I am the apple of God's eye you would treat me differently!" She was building momentum now, her voice rising. "You are spurning Gods chosen one when you look down on me!" The words shot through the air and whizzed through me with their familiar pain.

The culmination was at hand, the consequences imminent. "You are a hypocrite--full of evil thoughts and lies. A whitewashed tomb. Everything you do and say is a lie, and Satan is the father of lies, so you must belong to him!"

I could hear the cicadas buzzing outside. There had been a rash of them that summer, and when you walked on the lawn you could scarcely avoid the sickening crunch they made underfoot. I was aware that I was crying.

"Go to your room!" she ordered, flinging her arm out to point up the stairs. "I don't want to see you again, and I don't want you to talk to anyone. Have nothing to do with your sister either. This family will not associate with someone who refuses to re-spect those God has put in authority over them!"

I ran up to my room and lay across the bed, sobbing. I cried like this almost every day. I sometimes wondered if other kids cried all the time, but I didn't have anyone to compare myself to. Outsiders weren't welcome in our home. When they did gain access, after a brief honeymoon the relationship was always cut off because of "questionable motives" or a "spiritual oppression" they brought with them.

Even my little sister's friend, a seven-year-old, was forbidden to come to our home to play. The tears and pleas of my sister, eight years younger than I, did not sway the decision. Friends were not easy to come by under these circumstances, and though I was only partially aware of it, I lived an isolated, lonely life. I was less favored than my sister, and I never had a real friend at all. I told myself I didn't need friends, that I was fine the way I was. I deadened myself to the circumstances, neutralizing any hopes and expectations. I said "Whatever" a lot.

Mine was a precarious life as well as a lonely one. I was constantly on edge, vigilant, able to emotionally prepare myself instantly for what could come my way at any second. You learn quickly when the only thing predictable is the unpredictable.

We'd be packed and ready to go on vacation, only to cancel on the day of departure because the trip was "not God's will." We'd be eagerly anticipating a promised outing or gift, and it would be canceled or never delivered, again because of divine will. Pets were given away without discussion. We were dragged from church to church every couple of months, abandoning a congregation once the pastor said something that "disagreed with Scripture."

My father, a professor and theologian who was endlessly loyal to my mother, kept telling me it would get better, that God would do a new thing. He said this after each blowup, each tirade--and these could last for days.

I tried to believe him, and often after an eruption we experienced a period of calm. It was a scary calm--we weren't sure when things would flare up again--but it was a calm nonetheless, and I was grateful. Yet the pattern inevitably repeated itself, and despite our earnest prayers and hopes, nothing changed. My father sometimes bore his soul to me. "Why does she have to be so cruel to you?" he would say after an angry outburst that had left me shattered and sullen.

I didn't know.

"She not only puts the knife in," he said, "but she turns it."

The fighting between my parents was extreme. Screaming and door slamming woke me in the night. Days of tension paralyzed my sister and me with fear, and we crept quietly up to the attic to play with old toys.

"I need to rise above this," Dad would tell me in his vulnerable moments after he had been the target of an onslaught. "I have to not let what she does affect me."

Away from home (and he kept the two worlds very separate) my father's work and writing helped a great many people come to know the authentic power of Jesus at work in their lives. His combination of intellectual knowledge and conviction of the personal presence of God flooded the lecture halls where he spoke. But the world at home was scary, insane and lonely.

As I grew older, I discovered that my mother had been the victim of severe abuse as a child. Even though I intellectually began to come to terms with the reasons for her behavior, I was unable to free myself from her grasp. Still, my father's comments and judgments against my· mother's behavior helped me begin to grasp the unfathomable and experience a deep courage. Despite her claim that she was God's voice and presence in the world, despite her grandiose proposals and assertions about her power and unique giftedness, I began to realize that she was–perhaps– wrong.

Maybe these experiences were not God's will at all. Perhaps it was wrong that I couldn't have friends over or get involved in social activities. Maybe I wasn't born to be miserable all the time, and maybe I wasn't in the grips of Satan with evil spirits lurking in dark corners ready to oppress me and throw me into hell. Maybe I wasn't contaminated by those demons the way my mother said I was when she came into my room in the middle of the night to cast them out. Perhaps purging the house of evil - praying in each room that Satan would leave - was not the way most families spent their Saturdays.

At one point I suggested to my father that we get Mom some help. His usually gentle face went rigid and he sucked in his breath. He told me my mother didn't need help, that she was doing better, and he asked where my family loyalty was. He declared that God had given him this situation so he could learn to rise above it. Jesus suffered, saints suffered - why shouldn't he?

This topic was clearly taboo. It was just too painful for my father to identify the problem honestly. So the bizarre, erratic behavior continued to loom larger than life and define us. One day her tirade might be God's voice to shape us up. Another day a low mood was a "dark night of the soul" she was being called to walk through. She often believed her struggles were demonic and had many well-known people in the deliverance ministry try to cast out spirits from her. It never seemed to take. Other days she accused my father of having no faith and contaminating her with an oppression she could not shake off.

Years of intensive psychotherapy later, as I look back at the shattered landscape of my early life, I still shudder at the cycle of pain and abuse. The most chilling aspect of those years was the fact that my mother's spiritual language seemed to validate everything. Although I am sure there were spiritual components to my mother's condition, her ultra-spiritual terminology gave her assaults frightening leverage in our lives. If I had been able to grasp that my mother needed psychological help, perhaps I would not have taken her actions and words so much to heart. I would have had some mastery and control over the situation, and I would have had the correct words to define the reality in which I lived. Had my father been able to come to terms with the problem, I believe he would have attempted to persuade Mom to get professional help.

LEAVING HOME - WITH BAGGAGE

When I left for college, I watched from a distance as the situation became increasingly chaotic. During my visits home, I saw my dad's jovial demeanor dissolve into brooding melancholy. He began to question why he was still alive. One day as he was walking out of a bank, he fell over with a massive stroke and died. He was only in his sixties.

Mom eventually left the area, and her behavior continued to deteriorate, especially once my father was gone. His presence had served as a kind of support for her erratic condition; once he died, there was no one to contain it.

Our family's faith was a mixed blessing. Had we not believed in God, we might have sought help much more readily. Paradoxically, spiritual language can be a lacquer that covers over and justifies problems rather than helping us discern the most appropriate, even obvious, course of action.

REDEEMING MY PAST

I am a pastor now, and I see many people trapped in a similar cycle of pain. The woman in the abusive marriage whose husband threatens to kill her tells me, "Maybe if I just clean up that back room and keep the kitchen a little neater, things will get better. The Lord put me in this marriage, and God works all things for good." The wife of a bipolar man whose wild spending habits have brought them to financial ruin says, "God is telling me to love him and pray harder." There is certainly nothing wrong with loving, and praying harder is always warranted in difficult situations. But these people reappear in my office a week, a month, even a year or two later asking why God hasn't done anything. Despite their earnest prayers, heaven is silent. The old patterns keep repeating. There is no relief. In fact, the problem now looms larger than before.

I call this cycle "hamster-wheel suffering." In my work I have seen countless people who struggle with patterns of thought and behavior that keep them spinning but going nowhere. Unless we work through loss, trauma and abuse both psychologically and spiritually, we find ourselves muted, stymied and shut off from the present because of the past. The broad landscape of life grows dim and small. There seem to be no options. We cannot remember what used to bring us joy. Our sense of identity - if we ever had one - goes underground. Time collapses; we feel old or convince ourselves that life is almost over anyway. Dreams evaporate and fear interlaces even peaceful moments with dread. Delight, joy and wonder are replaced by obligation, guilt and routine.

When reading Dante's Inferno a while back I was struck by how much of the torment in Dante's hell is cyclical. The people in one group are all stabbed in the chest as they travel along their path. They continue on and their wounds begin to heal. As the bleeding stops, these sufferers find they have come full circle, and they are stabbed again. The healing effort is lacerated, and the cycle begins anew. Health and wholeness are dashed. The hope of a new thing is unrealized. This is the hamster wheel. This is hell on earth.

I know the hamster wheel. To seek God when you are in hell and not be able to find him is the most despairing journey of the human heart. Many people in this situation use spiritual language to cover their cyclical wounds, desperately trying to hold on to some sense of meaning and purpose. I do not look down on their efforts to find God in the midst of crisis and difficulty. Even after leaving home and breathing a big sigh of relief, I continued to relive the chaos I had grown up with. It was all I knew.

But now I know there is a difference between suffering that is cyclical and destructive and suffering that is redemptive. l realize that distinguishing between types of suffering can lead us to a potential Pandora's box of questions about evil and suffering in the world. To answer these questions is not the intent of this book. Nor do I assume that these distinctions are prescriptive

- set in stone. The distinctions I will be making are intended as general guidelines that can be applied practically so that people of God can be freed to recognize their purpose and not be shackled by endless patterns of futility and fear.

Throughout history the Enemy has used cyclical oppression to keep God's people enslaved, to keep them from recognizing the glorious purpose and hope to which they have been called. White slave owners in the Old South knew that once the African American slaves became educated, able to think and articulate their experiences, they would seek a higher form of life and recognize freedom as their inalienable right. So they passed laws forbidding anyone to teach slaves to read.

In the same way, if we stay blinded, uninformed and unable to understand or articulate what is happening to us, we cannot examine how our lives fall short of the glorious liberty we are entitled to as God's children. If we mistake the hamster wheel for God's will, we make God an oppressor rather than a liberator, a justifier, an outrageous forgiver and the Author of life. To live in freedom we must think intelligently about our lives and stay open to the possibility that things may not be as predetermined as we thought.

In the Gospels, Jesus does not succumb to every kind of suffering that comes his way. His identity as God's beloved Son and his sense of purpose and calling cause him to avoid certain situations. God reminds him before he goes into the wilderness to be tempted by the devil that Jesus is his beloved Son (Matthew 3: 17). This reminder of his identity as the beloved one is to encourage Jesus and build him up before a period of desolation. We too need to be reminded of who we are in the eyes of God. Paul tells us that we are chosen by God (Colossians 3: 12), his "beloved children" (Ephesians 5: l).

In the wilderness, Jesus knows who he is. There is no doubt in his mind, and he states it. The Enemy tries over and over to challenge this identity. "If you are the Son of God, let's see you prove it!" He distorts Scripture, and if Jesus were to follow what Satan wanted, he would come under the bondage and oppression of evil. But he doesn't. Time after time he answers Satan's distortions with statements of victory and purpose. When he emerges from the wilderness, his identity leads him to begin his ministry the right way. From the outset he tells people who he is and why he has come. He reads from Isaiah:

> The Spirit of the Lord is upon me,
> because he has anointed me
> to bring good news to the poor.
> He has sent me to proclaim release to the captives
> and recovery of sight to the blind,
> to let the oppressed go free,
> to proclaim the year of the Lord's favor. (Luke 4:18-19)

This is who Jesus is - the liberator of captives and the champion of the oppressed. He states to the people that this is his mission and call. And at first they think he's great. But when he refers to incidents in Scripture in which God intervened on behalf of non-Jews (Luke 4:24-27), implying that God has sent him to the Gentiles, they bring him to a cliff and prepare to hurl him over. How quickly they change! What does Jesus do? Stand there and let himself be destroyed? Does he say, "It must be God's will that I suffer for what I said. Go ahead, guys. I'll die a martyr right now by letting you toss me over this ledge!"

No. Scripture tell us, "He passed through the midst of them and went on his way" (Luke 4:30). On his way to where? To fulfill the purpose for which he came. Immediately he starts healing people, setting them free. The people love him so much they try to keep him from leaving them (Luke 4:42), but Jesus is clear about his call. He responds, "I must proclaim the good news of the kingdom of God to the other cities also; for I was sent for this purpose" (Luke 4:43).

Would you be able to succinctly sum up your call and your

reason for being sent to earth at this time? Are you able to spot scriptural distortions that perpetuate oppression rather than liberation? Are you able to act courageously and confidently in the truth that you have been beloved of God since the foundation of the world and are "of more value than many sparrows" (Matthew 10:31)? I know many Christians who don't feel worth one sparrow.

This book is about discovering your tremendous worth in Jesus Christ. It is meant to help you break out of the bondage that can steal your life and rob you of the purpose and call of God. In the following chapters I talk a lot about stopping the cyclical past in order to recognize God's liberation. The first crucial question to ask on this journey is, "Am I suffering because I am fulfilling my God-ordained call and purpose – or because I'm on a hamster wheel?"

To help in the discernment process, I try to give practical suggestions and examples, not a list of self-help solutions. This book is an effort to help you get in step with the Holy Spirit, the only true Helper, and discern his direction for your life. I encourage you to read prayerfully and seek the Holy Spirit's transformation. Recognizing patterns, remembering who Jesus is, and discovering the dreams God put deep inside you can open new channels for grace and change.

What I share with you on these pages is what I have lived. I am here now because of Jesus' love. Writing this book has made it necessary for me to turn myself inside out, exposing all my ragged edges and uneven seams. I have had to honestly examine the path my life has taken, including the many times my flaws and shortcomings got in the Lord's way. It has been necessary for me to assess what is holding me together these days and causing me to look forward to living rather than dying. So I share with you my insights, reflections and stories in hope that they might shed some light on who God is and who we as God's people are called to be in Christ Jesus. I start by describing the characteristics of hamster-wheel suffering, which we must recognize if we are going to be freed or help free those we love. The courage to change means we must dare to believe that although the hamster wheel is circling, there is a way out, a choice we can make that will launch us into a new way of living, loving, and allowing ourselves to be loved.

I hope you have a copy of the companion workbook (the *No More Running In Circles* workbook comes in both a participant and a leader's guide). It's a guide to help you personalize the principles I illustrate in this book. Based on the 12 steps, it is a twelve session study (intended for small groups) that I hope will guide you in your suffering, through your suffering, and eventually allow you to experience the grace of transformation that God invites us to experience. I believe the 12 steps offer us a pathway off the hamster wheel of suffering, and onto a journey of productive suffering that is transformative in nature. I pray that the workbook, along with this book provide you tools that help you find your way through your suffering...out of darkness, into the light.

Chapter 2

When the Suffering Becomes Unmanageable

Teresa McBean

Over twenty years ago, my brother acknowledged his addictions and entered a treatment facility in Atlanta, GA, after spending Christmas with our entire family at a fancy resort in Florida. It became apparent to him that his using was out of control. Neither he nor any other human can fully explain why, upon returning from our Christmas trip and trying unsuccessfully to kill himself with his drug of choice, he called my brother and said, "I need help." I personally think it was a God thing. The first step he took toward a recovered life was one of acknowledgment—I need help; my life is unmanageable.

One of my brother's first requests in treatment was for our family to get help along with him. I decided that the way I could support his recovery was by entering the meeting rooms myself, joining him in the 12-step work. My focus was on my codependency issues, but it soon became apparent to me that my battle with an eating disorder wasn't so different from my brother's obsession with cocaine. Upon realizing this, I also began to work the steps as a means to treat my own compulsivity. My brother wasn't the only one in our family with dependencies, powerlessness, and unmanageability issues; it was just that his out-of-control using was more obvious. My brother and I agree that our experiences with recovery are remarkably similar. Both of us believe that a large part of our collective work has focused around understanding self-deception and learning how to move beyond our denial. Denial is an amazing thing. It is exceedingly damaging and can be as fatal as too much crack. Our family's need for recovery is not unique—in fact, it's more common than we'd like to admit.

THE FIRST STEP

This was my brother's moment, and ultimately mine as well, to begin with the first step: We admitted that we were powerless over our dependencies and that our life had become unmanageable. (Details about how you can have your own step one experience are found in Kim's workbook, *No More Running In Circles*.)

The value of the 12-step work extends far beyond the assistance it provided my family in recovery from addiction and its effect on our family. My mother is currently coming to grips with a health diagnosis that no one wants to receive. My heartbreak over this dread disease and its ensnarement of my mom has been more over the denial around it than the actual disease itself (and that's saying a LOT because the disease is a nasty one). My family has struggled, as I understand is very common in situations like this, to acknowledge my mother's decline. Failure on our part to admit the reality of our situation has led to some consequences—medication messes, driving and getting lost, misunderstandings about why mom never calls us anymore, hurt feelings, and even the occasional temper tantrum (mostly that's me). We as a family have not been able to share our burdens openly because we have been trying to keep the obvious a secret. This has isolated us, made the burden heavier, and actually put our beloved mother and all other Atlanta drivers at risk. We're moving beyond denial into the truth, but it isn't easy.

A LIFELONG PROCESS WITH MANY OPPORTUNITIES TO LEARN

Working the 12 steps and applying these principles in all my affairs is helping me recover my life during this tragedy, just as they did so many years ago when I woke up to my codependent and eating disordered ways. Please do not think you need an addiction, or a mom with an illness, to propel you on the road to recovery. Even in the small things of daily living, we can wake up and discover that we have had a certain way of seeing that can induce spiritual sleepiness.

One summer I was going to be away from home for several

weeks in a row because of business commitments. I dreaded the time away from home. I'm not much of a traveler by nature. Simultaneously, and completely unconsciously, I began to obsess over all the times in the next few weeks when I would be forced to drink my morning coffee out of a foam cup. (It turns out that one of my favorite ritualistic dependencies is going down to the kitchen before the sun wakes up, picking a favorite mug and sipping a piping hot cup of coffee in peace and quiet.) My obsession over my loss of my morning routine resulted in me packing several mugs in my luggage. Problem solved? Well, not quite, because the problem really wasn't my morning coffee. My issue was that I was feeling uncomfortable and was asking for one of my dependencies to soothe my frazzled nerves—without actually having to deal with the root issue of my dis-ease. This is what dependencies promise us—a way around our underlying anxieties and secret fears, our unresolved issues, and childhood wounds. But dependencies cannot deliver on their promises, and that's one of the principles we'll learn as we walk through these steps.

My coffee mug obsession is a dependency and a symbol for me of my denial-prone tendencies. My longing for my morning ritual is somehow easier to obsess over than to acknowledge that my trip will cause me to miss my son's lacrosse game, my daughter's piano recital, and my husband's cuddly presence each night when I turn into bed after a long day. The way we distract ourselves from the "real deal" is harmful in two ways. First, the dependency/compulsion attachment is limiting. And, secondly, the failure to work through our real heart issues means that our growth and maturation process is stunted. (This topic will be developed further as we work through the steps.) For now, the key point is this: denial is a wall of limitation. It keeps us from naming our problem, which ensures that we are not free to find the solution. Admitting our powerlessness is the ticket out. Admitting that we have a problem drags it out of the darkness into God's wonderful light. God is in the business of rescue and recovery, but he's extremely respectful of our right to choose our own path. He won't violate our right not to want his awesome healing power.

In Abraham Twerski's book, *Addictive Thinking*, he stresses the danger of not addressing "the issue" as we employ various forms of self-deception. "I cannot stress enough the importance of realizing that addicts are taken in by their own distorted thinking and that they are its victims. If we fail to understand this, we may feel frustrated or angry in dealing with the addict."[1] Frankly, this is a human problem, not just an addict's issue. We all find various ways to deceive ourselves.

In the next chapter, Kim shares her story of suffering, and her experience with suffering unproductively. She uses a metaphor to describe this kind of suffering of a hamster running relentlessly on its wheel, moving fast but getting nowhere. It is stories like this that can open us up to consider taking that first step into a new way of seeing and responding to our suffering.

---

1. Abraham Twerski, *Addictive Thinking: Understanding Self-Deception* (Hazelton, 1997) p. 13.

Chapter 3

Recognizing the Hamster Wheel

Kim Engelmann

My marriage was a hamster-wheel marriage in which denial ran strong. We kept saying there was no problem. Our issues were a blip on the radar screen or a wrinkle in the fabric – but not a problem. I often didn't know where my husband, Tim, was for hours on end, we had heated arguments that were never resolved, and we failed to keep the promises we made each other - important promises. We were so fragmented and disorganized that the left hand didn't know what the right hand was doing. We didn't have many friends. Despite our dysfunction, I kept telling myself it wasn't so bad. And my life was still better than the craziness I had grown up with. I was trying so hard to hold everything together that I didn't see the patterns of my past emerging in my marriage. I thought I had gotten out. Instead I was repeating the old and familiar in a new way - and my marriage paid the price.

Realizing when we are in the hamster wheel is not easy. We lose ourselves in the cycling and think we are actually going somewhere. But clear distinguishing markers can help us identify when we are running in endless circles and then we can make a plan to get out. Some of the characteristics of hamster wheel suffering are outlined below.

HAMSTER·WHEEL SUFFERING IS SOLITARY

I have shared with you already that my family of origin functioned essentially in isolation from the outside world. This is often the case with abusive family systems. Many of the women I work with come to me because they are in abusive marriages, and isolation is a key weapon their abusers use to dis-empower them. I always try to link these women with a friend, a lay minister, or a counselor. In relationship they are able to find validation for their feelings and begin to see beyond the enclosed world that has become their existence. It was in relationship with a friend that I found the courage to persevere when I made extremely painful but necessary changes. It was her encouragement and that of the church where she was associate pastor that helped me stay out of the hamster wheel.

The importance of being in community with other Christians is an essential part of discerning God's will for our lives and following through on it. Community brings in the fresh aroma of new perspectives, ideas, and alternatives. I was struck the other day, as I read the Scripture, that before the Holy Spirit came, the disciples were "all together in one place" (Acts 2:1). This "togetherness" was the church. When the Holy Spirit came, the tower of Babel was reversed. All the people heard the gospel in their own language, and God drew them together under a common vision and message. The church was created so that we do not need to be alone, feeling as though no one understands. In community, we can validate and discern as well as celebrate. If you are suffering alone without people around you who can share, pray and celebrate with you, it may be that you are in a hamster wheel. No hamster ever runs in his wheel with another hamster. It is a solo endeavor.

People in destructive cycles are afraid of relationships. Even if we are not forced into isolation by an abusive spouse, our tendency to isolate becomes more extreme the more we feel marginalized by our circumstances. Once we begin to see our situation as worse than everyone else's, once guilt and self-hate enter in, it becomes easy to convince ourselves that we don't fit in and that our suffering makes us different from others. Given these erroneous assumptions, why would we even try to connect with anyone on the outside?

When I had a pet hamster, it ran on its wheel at night - squeak! squeak! squeak! - all evening long. Hamsters are nocturnal, becoming more active when the rest of the world is asleep. When it's us in the hamster wheel, the isolation we experience keeps us from seeing the light of day. Problems loom larger in our minds because we keep ourselves from others and don't benefit from their input—the light of their insight, so to speak.

One of our greatest sources of outreach at Menlo Park Presbyterian Church, where I once was a pastor, is a divorce recovery ministry. It is a weekly gathering of men and women who come together to share the pain of recent (or not so recent) divorce or separation experiences. Unfortunately, many people feel ostracized by the church after the breakup of a marriage. I think of my Catholic friend who was so afraid she would be damned that it took all her courage just to come and see me. But with this group, I look around the room and see people in dialogue with one another. I see heads bowed in prayer, hands grasped in friendship, and minds and hearts aware of the need for God. Tears are shed not in isolation, but in the presence of others. This community buoys up, validates and confirms, and teaches and corrects. Here is the church where people are "all together in one place," not just geographically, but psychologically and spiritually. It's a place where people recognize the frailty and brokenness of their own humanity and unabashedly acknowledge their absolute dependence on God.

Isolation is an attractive coping strategy for many people who have been disappointed by others, abused or neglected. We might call these individuals "survivors." Survivors who have made it on their own find it difficult to ask others for help. Survivors find it challenging to trust and allow themselves to be cared for. Survivors can be great caregivers, but not such great care receivers.

For a while I was in this category, going about my ministry with gusto. I couldn't receive in relationship; I could only give. And when you keep pouring a pitcher out onto dry ground, even if it's a pitcher with huge capacity, at some point that pitcher is going to dry up. I became aware through therapy that the care

I was giving to others was really the care I wanted someone to give to me. Learning to receive in relationship with others has been a great source of strength for me and is something I am still learning to do. It isn't easy. My tendency is to isolate, decide I don't need anyone, and wall others off when I am hurt or feeling blue. I know that this is not a healthy response, and after a time of being alone, I force myself to reach out. I do this because I know I need to trust and allow others to love and care for me even when I don't have it all together.

You get the sense from Paul, isolated in prison, that he longs for fellowship with others and that this longing comes from the core of his being. It is a passion, a deep desire, a gift from God. It isn't that he can't be alone. It's that the fellowship of believers gives him so much more joy and encouragement.

> I thank my God every time I remember you, constantly praying with joy in every one of my prayers for all of you, because of your sharing in the gospel from the first day until now. (Philippians 1:3-5)

> Therefore, my brothers and sisters, whom I love and long for, my joy and crown, stand firm in the Lord. (Philippians 4:l)

In order to be helped out of isolation into community, we need to have a desire and a willingness to receive in relationship. Receiving is core to the Christian message. We don't save ourselves. We receive or accept Christ into our lives. If we don't know how to receive from the brothers and sisters we can see, how can we hope to receive from a God we cannot see?

In his resurrection appearance, the very first thing Jesus asks his disciples to do is receive the Holy Spirit (John 20:22). In giving the Spirit he is breathing life on his disciples the same way he breathed life into Adam and Eve at the beginning of creation.

He's telling them to open themselves up to taking in the life of his presence. To open themselves up to taking in good things and letting them stick. To open themselves up to trust, hope, forgiveness, a new way of being, a new creation.

Openness requires vulnerability. That's what makes relationships a challenge for survivors. We might get hurt again. We might get lambasted, crushed or bruised. We've created good ways to avoid vulnerability, sheltering ourselves, and not entering fully into a life of relationship. That's why the hamster wheel is attractive - it's a solo endeavor. That's why the "me and Jesus" motif is attractive - we leave God's people out of the picture. But Paul called the people of God the very body of Christ. Live in isolation from others, and you live not knowing the tangible presence of Christ on earth. A sign of health and of trust in God is to surrender enough to open up and receive strength from others, especially from God's people--the church.

HAMSTER-WHEEL SUFFERING IS DEPLETING

When I would watch our pet hamster, Nugget, run in his wheel, there was no doubt that he was getting a true little hamster workout. No one was making that wheel turn but him. If isolation is the first sign of hamster-wheel suffering, then Herculean effort is the second. It is necessary to put forth a tremendous amount of energy to keep things moving and perpetuate the destructive cycle. The rhythmic lull of life as we know it, as we have always known it, keeps us running in the wheel when we ought to let it stop.

"I have to stay with him," a woman told me recently. "I have to stay because my pastor told me that if I left I would be disobeying God, and I wouldn't go to heaven. He told me that I am probably not the wife l should be, and that's why my husband beats me. Besides, if I left it would destroy my husband's Christian witness. He's an evangelist, you know. I think I just need to try harder to be a good wife."

This is an extreme example of hamster-wheel suffering. This woman lived an isolated life with no transportation and no outlets for herself. She was making a Herculean effort to please. She was constantly trying harder--to not burn the roast, to keep the children tidy and quiet. It was amazing she had made it to my office at all.

"It will happen again," I told her. "There will always be something wrong. No matter how hard you try, you will not be able to please him. You've got to get out of there."

She didn't believe me. She shook her head, and I think she thought I was terribly un-Christian to suggest such a thing. Six months later she was back. Nothing had worked. Eventually, with some encouragement and a concrete plan put into place with the help of some wonderful women at our church, she found freedom from the abusive cycle. Now she sits with other women and uses her experience to free them from the pain of abuse. If she had kept trying on her own steam to keep the wheel turning, she probably would not be alive today. If her husband had not killed her, she would have collapsed either emotionally or physically from sheer exhaustion.

One of the things I ask people I perceive to be in the hamster wheel is how they're doing physically. Often the stress of running around and around, going nowhere, has taken its toll on their limbs, joints, and organs. No one can sustain continued grief, pain, stress and trauma without physical effects. Nor is it God's will that anyone be destroyed by their circumstances. But if you don't stop the wheel from turning, if you don't give up the solo show of holding everything together, gradually you will be destroyed.

When I was a child, I felt even at a young age that I had to hold it together for my parents. As a result I was sick all the time. Allergies, strep throat and chronic ear infections plagued me. Our family doctor would look at me and shake his head, saying, "I sure wish I could give you a new nose."

My nose was stuffed up all the time. By the time I was an adult the pattern of chronic sickness was ingrained. Feeling exhausted and depleted was part of life.

"I just can't do it anymore," people often tell me. "But if I don't keep going, everything will fall apart." Sometimes it's just fine to let things fall apart--before you do--because then it becomes possible to rebuild.

There are a hundred and one reasons we can give for why we must keep the hamster wheel turning. "It wouldn't be good for the kids." "There's not enough money." "What will people think?" "I can't change my life; it's chaotic enough as it is." These cycles of thinking rob us of the energy we need to go in a new direction—the energy to discover God's call and purpose for our lives.

Stopping the hamster wheel can be painful, much the way hitting bottom is painful for an alcoholic. Our joints may ache. Our lives may feel empty without all the frenetic activity. There's no doubt that getting out of the wheel takes courage. It requires a stalwart trust that God will see us through the lonely, unfamiliar times and provide the deep healing we crave at the center of our being.

If you are depleted at the end of each day and wake in the morning with little capacity to enjoy or anticipate, chances are you are running in that rodent wheel. With the help of others and with Jesus holding your hand, you can take a leap of faith and get out.

HAMSTER·WHEEL SUFFERING GOES NOWHERE
When we're in the hamster wheel, we continually find ourselves right back where we started. This is obvious to the outside observer; anyone can tell you the hamster ends up in the same place he was when he began. But it's not so obvious to us. We think we're being diligent and intense in our endurance of difficulty, but in the end we go absolutely nowhere.

The Enemy loves distortion, and if he can get us to think that we're going somewhere for the kingdom of God when we're actually going nowhere at all, he has successfully distracted us from the reason we were created: to glorify God and enjoy him forever.

If we assume that all suffering is constructive and fail to discern that we are in a self-destructive cycle, we risk missing out on God's plan to give us a "future with hope" (Jeremiah 29:11) --a plan that takes us somewhere. Again, Jesus didn't succumb to every kind of suffering. When that mob of angry people tried to push him off the cliff, he passed through them and went on his way. Jesus knew that his life would eventually be sacrificed, but the time was not now. It may be hard for us to come to terms with the reality that we are going nowhere. It may seem to us, as we are caught up in the dizzying frenzy of the hamster wheel, that we are making great progress. This often happens to people we might consider to be very successful. One high-level corporate executive told me, "I made it to the top and found there was nothing there."

The longing of our lives, deep at the core, has nothing to do with self-made success. It has everything to do with finding our God-given call: our divinely appointed reason for being in the world.

Chapter 4

A Gracious Intrusion

Kim Engelmann

As I have shared with you, my early family life made me question whether I had a purpose or call at all. I wondered why I was alive. I thought about killing myself often, and my mood was flat and depressed.

As a teenager, I was headed south. I wanted to believe in God, but I had been told many times that God was out to get me, and my image of him was distorted by false language that made his nature murky and frightening. One afternoon when I was thirteen, I was feeling desperate and alone. My parents had separated, and my mother had whisked my sister and me across the country to a new school in the middle of the year.

Without the fragments of my father's love and concern, I was in a deep depression. I was failing science in an unfamiliar school. I was convinced I was fat and ugly. And I had just found out that my parents had given my dog away. I loved that Sheltie, and the rage and sorrow that welled up in me after overhearing the news (no one told me directly) took the last teaspoon of pluck out of me. Sitting on the couch in the living room, I began to cry. This in itself was not unusual, but this time I couldn't stop. It was as if I was being sucked down into an abyss. I was out of strength and didn't have one bit of tenacity left.

DIVINE INTERVENTION

The truth is that so often when we are at our lowest ebb, when we have nothing left, it seems to oil the hinges for the door of God's presence to swing magnificently wide, allowing us to experience the reality of God's presence in a whole new way. For me, in that moment on the couch, the song "Amazing Grace" crackling out over the radio, sung by the old-time voice of

George Beverly Shea, oiled those hinges. What I experienced as I only half-listened to the familiar hymn hit me broadside. It pulled me up and caught me by surprise. It stopped my tears, but then started them again for an entirely different reason. I was overcome with the presence of Jesus.

As I sat there, I was flooded with a delighted, almost chuckling love that rippled through my being like a river. Wave after wave of it poured through me; I couldn't stop it. I had the sense that the joy and warmth and aliveness was endless and that I was eternally held in that reality. This was not the God I knew, the one who was distant, disapproving and coercive, the one who chewed people up and spit them out. This was a God who longed to be in relationship with me. I had the sense that I was known, that my name was acknowledged, that this Someone who knew me (did I dare call this One by that awful name God?), had allowed my life to have meaning. I wasn't a forgotten bit of froth tossed up by a wave and left to evaporate on the sand. In the loving gaze of this Someone, I was an eternal being who was infinitely more important and valuable than I had ever believed.

That night I stayed up all night and read Scripture. The words jumped off the page and walked around with new life. I was transfixed by the fact that as I read the Bible I no longer felt condemned but outrageously and fervently cared for. This was a love that any human love I had experienced up to that point couldn't even begin to approach. Even at 48 years old, when I go back to that moment, it defines who God is for me.

I told this story once in a sermon and was jolted by the responses of the people after the service. I must have heard similar accounts at least ten times over the course of three services that morning. With tears in their eyes, people said things like, "I know what you mean. When I was very young I had an experience of Jesus' love, and I've never forgotten it. Life has been hard, but I keep remembering Jesus' love the way I experienced him back then." The magnificence of Jesus' presence is unforgettable. It touches everything we long for as humans. You don't forget Jesus' presence. You can't.

When I was young, I lived in Switzerland for a year with my family. If you followed the road we lived on up the hill, you would come to a large field along one side. The villagers who lived in that area told us that, on a clear day, there was a magnificent view of Mount Blanc across this field. Mount Blanc was the highest of the Swiss Alps, but try as we might, we couldn't catch a glimpse of it. Every time we drove up there, the mist hung low and the clouds were heavy, and all we saw was an empty field. After a while we stopped journeying that way, thinking that perhaps the view was overrated, an exaggeration meant to trick naive Americans into renting houses close by.

But then one day early in the morning, we traveled up that hill again. This time the mists were gone, and there the mountain stood. A great jagged peak was soaring up to the sky, flashing reds and pinks from the rising sun. It was glorious, and we marveled. We made many more travels to that field after that, and most of the time the view was obstructed by mist. But we had seen that alpine giant once and the vision stayed with us. Occasionally it greeted us again with grandeur, but even when we couldn't see it, we knew it was there.

Many people have had an experience of God's presence, and they know he is there. Sometimes they are estranged from him for a long time, but they come back to him. They come back because they remember. They remember when the mist lifted, when they knew Jesus was real, when the reality of his presence was so magnificent that it stuck.

One man shared with me that he'd had a grandmother who rocked him to sleep at night, singing 'Jesus Loves Me,' when he was three years old. He had become a successful man, competent in every way the world deems important. Yet he remembered his grandmother singing to him in the cauldron of an argumentative, atheistic home with parents who told him God was a crutch. "I felt God's presence," he said. "As she sang, I was aware that there was something more than this life." This experience eventually brought him back to church in his forties, with his own children in tow.

When God's presence enters our meager four-score-and-ten existence, as we hack it out by the sweat of our brow, it is something we remember for the rest of our days. It resonates with the deepest part of who we are, because it is what we were created for. It chimes out, "The one who is in you is greater than the one who is in the world" (1 John 4:4). It is a vital reference point in our spiritual walk, and it keeps refreshing us and bringing us new life. This gracious intrusion into the way we think, the way we live, the way we create our world pulls us out of our distorted thinking and brings new life to the way we describe God.

I get criticized for being a grace fanatic. I get pinned to the wall at times by those who think I spend too much time talking about the love of God. I can't help it. It's all I know. I was rescued from hell on earth, from atheism, from suicide, by this Eternal Lover, and to not talk about it would be disastrous. To go back to being motivated by fear, by works, by climbing a ladder to try to please God with my filthy-rags righteousness would be a slap in the face to the One who calls me to live from a place of gratitude, forgiveness and adoration of Jesus.

Do you see how the wrong kinds of spiritual language can distort the image of God and make it difficult to get out of the hamster wheel? This is why we have so many joyless Christians walking around. They've forgotten who God is! They've forgotten or have never known "the deep, deep love of Jesus, vast, unmeasured, boundless, free," as the old song puts it. They've been duped by angry preachers, condemning parents, or critically spiritual people who point out weaknesses in others for their own self-aggrandizement.

The wrong kinds of spiritual language create horrible idolatries, which we worship without even realizing it. Our image of God, the picture we have of him, is vital for our freedom in Christ. It is vital for our joy in Christ. It is vital for getting out of the hamster wheel. Ask yourself, "Am I worshiping the God of Jesus Christ, or am I worshiping some other god that was created in my own mind by legalism or punishment?"

Until we are transformed by the Holy Spirit our tendency is to create God in our own image based on past experiences, human interactions, and our horizontal world. The Israelites made the golden calf by melting their jewelry. They created an idol from the stuff of their lives. They made it from what they had acquired in the world. What did they come up with? A cow! Moo. Couldn't they have come up with something a little more transcendent? If you are going to make an idol, folks, at least do something inspiring.

But we are no better. When we create God from the stuff of our experiences in this world, when we meld together a conglomerate of what we accumulate in this life, we are bound to come up with a pretty sorry representation of God[2]. That is why preachers and teachers and all Christian leaders must use language that adequately expresses who God is in the person of Jesus Christ. Jesus is called the Word of God. He is the divine expression of love poured out lavishly without limit. He is the very essence of God's heart. He is the eternal transcendent, one who is without end in his mercy and compassion and ebullient, self-sustaining, resurrection joy. The words we use can remind us again and again of this truth. "The truth will make you free," Jesus tells his disciples (John 8:32). And what is truth? To know God and his Son, Jesus Christ. The knowledge of God's nature in its wonderful reality can free us from the shackles of idolatry.

---

2. For a more in-depth study on this subject, the *Restoring our Vision* bible studies written by Dale and Juanita Ryan are excellent resources. Both *Distorted Images of Self* and *Distorted Images of God* can be purchased through Amazon.

Jesus had tremendous distaste for the ways the words of Scripture were used to validate oppression and human suffering. Look at what he does with the interpretation of "Remember the Sabbath day, and keep it holy" (Exodus 20:8). He goes out and heals people on the Sabbath, setting them free from illness and disability--to the chagrin of the scribes and Pharisees (John 7). He wasn't supposed to do that! But I can just see Jesus shaking his head in frustration. "This law was made for you! You weren't made to keep this law!" The dos and don'ts of Scripture are meant for freedom, not for hamster-wheel futility.

Jesus' ministry was focused on undoing the misinterpretation of Scripture. The disciples stand by, wide-eyed, and stammer, "But ... but ... you're not supposed to do that!" The Pharisees are even more surprised--and outraged. "You're not supposed to heal on the Sabbath, or set that prostitute free. The law says she has to be stoned. You aren't supposed to care about Samaritans or touch lepers. The words in the law say they are unclean! You aren't supposed to say that you are God-that's blasphemy!"

God's Word made flesh was a profound revelation that we had managed to use to distort God and keep people in bondage, running around in a hamster wheel, serving a God made up of our own stuff and in our own image.

From Exodus to Revelation God is constantly appearing to set his people free... Look! You're not slaves anymore; here's the Promised Land. Look! You've got Jesus; here I am to die for you so you don't have to sacrifice anymore. Look! Here's the Holy Spirit to empower you to live in freedom. Look! Someday I will set things right, and there will be no more suffering and sighing. Don't succumb to legalism--a system based on fear. Don't let laws be your security; instead let my love keep you safe, secure, and liberated.

In the Sermon on the Mount, Jesus declares, "You have heard that it was said ... but I say to you ... " (Matthew 5:21-43). Jesus is declaring his divinity by rewriting the Mosaic Law. He is calling people to conform to a pattern of grace and freedom, which was the intent of the law to begin with.

Since so much of Jesus' ministry was focused on reinterpreting the intent of the words of Scripture, redefining our image of God and helping people to see that "God so loved the world," it seems that the church ought to sit up and take notice. How does spiritual language create a distorted image of God and keep us in the hamster wheel?

Each week in our workbooks we practice noticing the symptoms of hamster-wheel language. Recognizing this language can help set us free. But the ultimate healing power comes from an experience of God's presence. After my own miraculous encounter with the love of Jesus, my struggles were far from over. The difference, however, was that I knew who God was, and I could keep going back to that liberating experience again and again as a reference point. I could begin to believe that I was loved and that maybe, even for me in the dark tunnel of my childhood, there was a future and a hope.

Chapter 5

Taking the Next Right Step

Teresa McBean

At one of Kim's lowest points, she was overcome by an awareness of the presence of Jesus. Certainly Kim already knew a lot about Jesus; her father was a theologian, and her mom often spoke of God in ways that were confusing and abusive but certainly left no room for doubt that God exists. But knowing that there is a God—even knowing and feeling very confused about what that means—isn't the same as actually experiencing the loving, gracious presence of God, which is what Kim wrote about in the previous chapter.

Kim's encounter with God (her "coming to believe" experience) awakened within her the possibility that perhaps what she had heard from her family about God wasn't accurate. She warns us of the danger of creating God in our own image (or in the image of one of our parents). It is this careless "languaging" of spiritual things that presents a challenge for some of us who have been exposed to a certain perspective on God rather than an experience with God.

When I hear Kim's story, I am touched by how a lonely little girl, in an instant, is given the gift of God's presence. Coming to believe for me was not that dramatic or instantaneous, but the steps I took in a moment of great desperation was no less powerful. I learned this: I am not alone. The 12-step model, which was helpful for my spiritual awakening, taught (and continues to teach) me that I have neither the power nor the responsibility for the care and proper management of others. And even in those situations when I find myself participating in problem solving, there is a power greater than those of us struggling to seek solutions, and this power is beneficent and restorative.

THE SECOND STEP

In a nutshell, at this moment in the process, that's all these early steps are asking us to consider.

Next, we'll proceed to step two: We came to believe that a power greater than ourselves could restore us to sanity. (Check out the workbook for more information.)

Notice the verb tense—it's saying we "came to believe," meaning we don't have to have this "higher power stuff" all figured out. It is simply asking us to realize that there is a God, and we didn't get the job. We are not God. For me, that was part of my most profound work in step two. I had to tell the truth—I am not God. I am not able or willing to know all, do all, or figure all of life out for myself and for others.

This step doesn't require us to have a lot of faith—just the willingness to be made willing. We were created to be and to do much more than live a life of quiet desperation. As we move through this step, we need to know that we are not alone. Others are praying for us. God tells us that He will redeem our life from the pit. From a former pit dweller, let me assure you—when God says He will do it, it will be done!

PROCESS, NOT A PROGRAM; EXPERIENCE, NOT KNOWLEDGE ALONE

"Coming to believe" is a process. We move from giving lip service to God's existence to a belief that I call "knowing that you know that you know." We were not created to live in a vacuum of unbelief. We were created to believe. It is part of the "eternity in our hearts" described by the author of Ecclesiastes:

> I have seen the burden God has laid on men…He has also set eternity in the hearts of men; yet they cannot fathom what God has done from beginning to end. Ecclesiastes 3:10-11.

As the writer of Ecclesiastes points out, this belief is a messy, complex thing. That's why coming to believe is a process! Unless we grapple with the existence of the unseen world, it is my firmly held conviction that we cannot live well in the seen world. Most of us have been cheated out of our belief and the abundant life that accompanies radical believing. It is like our capacity to believe has been stolen. Jesus put it this way: "The thief comes only to steal and kill and destroy; I have come that they may have life, and have it to the full" (John 10:10). Our pasts have left many of us hurt and damaged. We're in bondage to a lot of lies—misuse of religion, cultic experiences, traditions that run counter to God's truth—and these harmful exposures leave us scarred. In these early steps, we won't have to get all that figured out. Now is the time to do three things (as suggested by Mike O'Neill in his book, *Power to Choose*):

1. Figure out what we truly believe.
2. See if our belief is false or true.
3. Decide to believe that which is true.

"I know what I'm doing. I have it all planned out—plans to take care of you, not abandon you, plans to give you the future you hope for. When you call on me, when you come and pray to me, I'll listen. When you come looking for me, you'll find me. Yes, when you get serious about finding me and want it more than anything else, I'll make sure you won't be disappointed." (Jeremiah 29:11-14, The Message)

In the next chapter, Kim is going to continue a discussion of how false spirituality keeps us stuck on the hamster wheel. She is going to provide us some ways to articulate why, perhaps, we are hesitant to trust talk about "God stuff"—why our talk about God might not match our daily life experience with God. Alcoholics Anonymous (AA) has a saying, "Nothing changes if nothing changes." So open yourself up to the possibility that what you think you know about God might not be accurate. (Conversely, confusion over who God is might also leave us confused about who we are too!)

Chapter 6

How False Spirituality Keeps Us Stuck

Kim Engelmann

The language we use creates much of the reality in which we live. Language expresses our state of mind, and when we share it, it shapes another person's state of mind. Just as God created the world through his word, so our words create our world. The difference is that God's words create only life and beauty because God is all good. We, on the other hand, have the capacity to create both life and death with our words. We can destroy others with our words.

Words were a big deal in my family growing up, often used to tear down rather than build up. Some people ask incredulously why I am still a Christian, and I agree that given the past distortions of faith I experienced, I shouldn't be. For a while, as a preteen, I decided I didn't believe in God. I wanted to get out and stay out of all that nonsense. God seemed to operate the way my family did: with the chewing gum approach. Chew on people for a while to experience all their flavor and consistency and then, once you've depleted them of taste and elasticity, spit them into the trash can.

My image of God was created by words that motivated me to respond to God out of fear. "If you don't comply with my wishes and demands, God will not bless you," I heard again and again. "God told me that you have evil thoughts in your heart toward me. No one who has evil thoughts toward me will escape God's judgment." If something good happened to me, I was told, "Beware when all men speak well of you," and "The first shall be last." These words terrified me. Who would want to have anything to do with God after such messages of gloom? Thank goodness for my experience of Jesus' love. This gracious intrusion into the abusive cycle redefined everything.

The wrong kind of spiritual language can keep us stuck in the hamster wheel a long time. It can produce feelings of guilt, obligation, and shame that distort the image of God. We can use it to protect ourselves when we don't want to get in touch with our pain. Sometimes we don't know what to do, so instead of being honest, we resort to lingo that is safe and familiar. Following are some types of spiritual language that keep us from being genuine with ourselves and others, that keep us from recognizing our call and purpose, and most importantly, that keep us distant from who we are and who God is.

THE LANGUAGE OF DENIAL

Spiritual language can be used to help us deny that a problem exists. Denial is a fine mode of protection. It keeps pain out of our mind. It holds at bay what we do not wish to remember. It is a survivor's shield that we can hold in front of our faces to block our view of the horrific landscape around us.

People often talk about denial in a condescending way, as if it were something to be ridiculed. But denial has helped me cope at certain points in my past. There is a strong benefit to defenses that preserve our sanity; sometimes confronting an issue head-on would wreck us emotionally. There is a time to be in denial, but there is also a time to work through the pain little by little, as much as we can handle at any one time. Once we name the problem, we are ready to get off the hamster wheel.

Denial was the primary tool that I used to stay on the hamster wheel even after I was married. Since my mother's problems hadn't been owned or recognized, I found it difficult to own or recognize that Tim and I had problems. The first step to getting off the hamster wheel is acknowledging that you even have a problem. I wasn't able to do this for a long time. I didn't want to look at the pain in my past or acknowledge my present relational mess. I wasn't even sure I had permission to call it bad.

What if there was no problem?

What if it was just in my head? Or what if I was exaggerating an issue that was no big deal?

I once sat with someone who had lost a loved one. She kept saying, "God works all things together for good," and the spiritual lingo helped her to be present in a situation that was so painful she could hardly bear it.

After our first meeting, I finally said, "You know, it's awful that your loved one died. It must be very hard for you to pray right now. Why don't you let me do your praying for a while?" At this point the woman burst into tears. Gently we began to talk about the grief and loss that was just under the surface.

Many of us use spiritual lingo to remain in denial so that everything stays fine, shallow and nice. The church can be a perpetrator of the fine, the shallow and the nice; our hollow spiritual language acts as a gloss that covers the ugly stuff. Perhaps one of the reasons churches breed this kind of coping strategy is that we feel have to defend God when something bad happens. Admitting the anguish that we feel might mean that God is not faithful.

It's funny that we do this in churches, because the Bible doesn't sugarcoat things at all. It is ruthlessly honest, raw and real. When the psalmist is in trouble, instead of saying, "Well, all things work together for good," he cries out with despair.

> "Will the Lord reject forever?
> Will he never show his favor again?" (Psalm 77:7 NIV).

> "My heart is in anguish within me" (Psalm 55:4 NIV).

> "My God, my God, why have you forsaken me?
> Why are you ... so far from the words of my groaning?"
> (Psalm 22:1 NIV).

"How can I go on? Why do you let terrible things happen to the people you love?" he asks God. This kind of honesty testifies to a relationship with God that's so strong it doesn't need to be protected. God holds on to us and preserves us. We do not preserve God.

THE LANGUAGE OF MINIMIZATION
The language of minimization is something we use to neutralize the negative charge of an oppressive hamster-wheel situation.

"It's not so bad," we tell ourselves.

Churches are rife with this kind of thinking because many of them teach, directly or indirectly, that Christians shouldn't have problems --if they do, somehow it's their own fault. God ought to be enough. If they had more faith, prayed more regularly or memorized more Scripture, their problems would vanish. In order for these people to feel that they are good Christians, they must minimize their issues and keep them insignificant in their mind. Sound familiar? And how often have we done this to ourselves? We wonder, in the middle of a sleepless night, is this all my fault? Is God trying to get my attention? Am I being punished?

Nowhere in Scripture do we see someone praying to God and God telling them, "It's no big deal. Buck up and stop whining." In fact, Jesus speaks about how God clothes the lilies, cares even about what we wear and eat, and considers each day of our lives important (Matthew 6:28; Luke 12:27). He encourages us to share our concerns with him (Philippians 4).

Children know this instinctively. Their smallest concerns get shot up to God in prayer at bedtime. "Graham was mean to me." "I lost my hamster, please help me find him." "Give me a friend." "Help there not be peanut butter for lunch." Jesus said that God cares even when a sparrow dies and that he loves us far more than the birds (Matthew 10:31). What happens to us, what causes us pain, is held much more closely to God's heart than we know. Nothing is minimized in God's economy.

But minimization can escalate out of control when problems are immense and we simply don't know how to deal with them. This kind of coping occurred in the following interaction I had with a man, Rod, who wanted to talk about a situation. Rod kept telling me it was "nothing." See what you think.

"Well, here I am," Rod said as he came in the door. "I finally got in the office to see you. I'm sure you have a lot of other people to see, so I'm sorry to take up your time."

"It's time that I had set aside for you," I said. "I'm glad you're here, and I have almost an hour for us to talk. How are you doing?"

"I don't have to take long. I just wanted to let you know that I have lymphoma. I mean, it's nothing new. I've had it for a long time but now it's stage four and I'm feeling a little depressed. I'd just like a quick prayer."

"That's terrible. I am so sorry."

"Yeah, well, as I said, it's been a long road. Nothing new."

"I bet. Did you know we have a men's cancer support group that meets here? It's a bunch of guys that get together, pray and talk through what it's like to have a long-term disease that can make you feel sick for extended periods of time."

"Well, it's not that I can't deal with it. I mean, I think of all the poverty in the world, and people who are really suffering. My mother had a bad liver and a heart problem. My brother, well, he's been divorced and has an addiction problem. I'm happily married, have two great kids, and I've had a good life so far. I'm grateful for that. And I feel guilty for feeling depressed and lethargic when I may not have that much longer to . . . be around."

I looked at him and for a moment we were silent.

"It is not a small matter to be in stage four cancer," I finally said. "This is a big deal. You've got a lot of concerns inside that you may want to talk about. I can't even imagine the turmoil you must be in. Are you concerned for your wife? For your kids?"

This comment was all he needed. Rod nodded, choked up and began to tell me what was really going on. He felt abandoned by God. He didn't like being sick. He wanted to be healed. He thought that by not making a "big deal" of things he was having faith and that this would ensure his healing. He was also lonely. We had a good talk and a long, heartfelt prayer. He agreed to go to the support group. He would also get prayer from a team designed to pray for healing. I offered him some other counseling options as well.

Minimization of his problem was a way for Rod to cope with the overwhelming sorrow of his situation and the worry that his illness might separate him from his wife and children. It was necessary for him to keep the brutal reality at arm's length just so he could function. And by trying not to dwell on the underside of things, Rod thought he was having more faith and perhaps would be more likely to experience healing. But all this minimization was masking an intense desperation in Rod's heart and preventing him from receiving the support and understanding he needed.

I find it interesting when I read Scripture to note that when Jesus commends people by saying, "Your faith has made you whole," he doesn't equate the word faith with the ability of people to minimize a problem. Actually, the people Jesus commends are those who are doing precisely the opposite. They know they have a big problem, and because they know it, they make great efforts to reach out to Jesus. Like the woman with the flow of blood, who is well aware that Jesus is the only one who can help her. No minimization here, just honest human desperation. As people acknowledge their weakness and dependency, Jesus meets them.

I see minimization often with spouses who live in violent situations, like the woman who said to me, point blank, "Well, it's only the first time he's pulled the phone out of the wall and broken a window. He's under a lot of stress at work. It's not like he curses at the children all the time. It's really not so bad."

Jesus never minimizes. He sees the cruelty of the world, and he feels the pain of others deeply. He cries at Lazarus' tomb (John 11:35). He invites people who are "weary and carrying heavy burdens" to come to him (Matthew 11:28), and he has compassion on those who are like "sheep without a shepherd" (Matthew 9:36). He calls our generation "faithless and perverse" (Matthew 17: 17) and anguishes over going to the cross because he knows how hellish it will be to feel the weight of the sins of the world on his shoulders. He is, according to Isaiah, "a man of suffering and acquainted with infirmity" (Isaiah 53:3). Brennan Manning says, in *The Ragamuffin Gospel*,

When we speak of Jesus Christ as Emmanuel, God with us, we are saying that the greatest lover in history knows what hurts us. Jesus reveals a God who is not indifferent to human agony, a God who fully embraces the human condition and plunges into the thick of our human struggle. There is nothing Jesus does not understand about the heartache that hangs like a cloud over the valley of history. In His own being He feels every separation and loss, every heart split open with grief, every cry of mourning down the corridors of time.

If Jesus felt the rawness of humanity and cried out, "My God, my God, why have you forsaken me?" then certainly we too can have confidence that coming face to face with our own sorrow is a part of life, a part of healing, a part of being genuine and honest before God. God knows our hearts and sees beneath our coping strategies to the raw pain there. Perhaps by becoming more honest with ourselves we draw nearer to the mind of Christ.

LANGUAGE THAT FORCES AN OPPOSITE REACTION

We use opposite-reaction language when we decide that God, or people, or the Bible will not allow us to feel a certain way. "I'm not supposed to feel bad, so I'm going to feel good," we say, putting all the energy we want to use to kick the dog into petting the dog instead. The dog is still ticking us off, but we simply flip a switch and make ourselves act the opposite of how we feel.

This kind of language was rampant in the seventies with a Christian movement that declared that no matter what happened, all we had to do was "praise the Lord." If we did, everything would work out all right. Many churches still promote this perspective in varying degrees. If we "stay positive" somehow we can then control God with our great faith. The Bible does say to rejoice in all circumstances (Philippians 4:4), but it also says to "weep with those who weep" (Romans 12:15). A forced positive response works for a while, but eventually the ugly stuff seeps out in other ways. Faith is a gift, not a way to force a desired outcome.

THE LANGUAGE OF AVOIDANCE

I remember sitting with a woman whom I absolutely wanted to throttle. (I realize that this is not exactly a pastoral attitude.) I cared deeply for this woman and wanted to see her get her life on track, but she kept using spiritual lingo to keep herself safe and distant from what was really going on. The lingo allowed her to avoid getting the help she needed, and it was clear from my standpoint that she was close to a nervous breakdown. Our conversation went something like this.

"Jenny, I'd like to refer you to a counselor who is a wonderful person, whom I deeply respect, and who will be able to help you work through some of the things you've shared with me today."

"I've already been to counseling. I know what they say, and they don't help. I've read a bunch of books, but they don't help either. It's only the Lord who can help."

"That's for sure. God is the only one who can really help, and in a minute we'll pray and ask for help. But sometimes we need someone with 'skin on' to sort out the pain of our past. It's not head knowledge that we're after, here; I think you need heart knowledge of what you already know in your head."

"Well, God has told me that I don't need counseling. All I need to do is pray. I'm signing up for this Christian conference on prayer. I think it's what the Lord wants me to do."

She patted a brochure and nodded as if to reassure herself that she had the answer.

"I think it will be a good conference, and I hope you get a lot out of it," I responded, trying to affirm her effort. I knew it was hard for her to take initiative. "But I know you go to a lot of conferences and you hear a lot of really good speakers. Somewhere all this good stuff is getting lost in the transfer because you still aren't able to live the way you want to live - the way the speakers tell you how you are 'supposed' to live, and life still is very burdensome for you."

Jenny shifted uneasily in her chair and got a little teary.

"It is very hard," she mumbled.

Oh, good. We're finally getting somewhere, I thought.

"But," she said, looking up at me suddenly with a smile as glossy as the brochure she was holding, "I'm fine. Jesus said, 'Ask and you will receive,' and that is what I am going on. I don't need anyone. All I need is the Lord."

"Jenny," I tried one last time. "The Lord has given us one another to help us get through the hard times. And by the looks of it, you are going through a pretty hard time right now."

"So did a lot of people in the Bible. 'Blessed are you who are persecuted for righteousness' sake,'" she declared like a little parrot. "Well, that's what it is. I am being persecuted and no one understands this unless they are spiritually minded. Someday I'm going to get my reward and that's what I'm waiting for."

I prayed with Jenny. I continue to pray for her. As the years have come and gone, Jenny has stayed immobilized. She hasn't changed. I see her cycle in and out of episodic depression. I see her looking blankly at me during worship. I see her alone, her hair greasy, her clothes disheveled.

In contrast, there are some in our church who readily admit that they suffer from a mental illness. It is healing for me to work with people who are honest about their difficulties. Accurately naming the problem has helped them live their lives with an openness and vulnerability that invites others into their experience. They have formed a fellowship group called HELP (healing, encouragement, love and prayer) with more than two hundred people on the mailing list. HELP meets once a week to share a meal, have devotions and most of all pray for one another. I have never seen such fervent prayers. These people don't need a curriculum. They don't need cutesy gimmicks to keep them interested. All they want to do is pray, and it is to them that I give urgent prayer requests when I have them.

Many of the folks who struggle with mental illness have unabashedly declared their utter dependence on God. One woman in particular has testified in church how Jesus was present with her in the midst of a hospitalization for clinical depression. She saw Jesus walking her out of darkness and bringing her into a lighter place. "I still struggle," she said to the four thousand people who came to worship that weekend. "I know I am weak. But God is my strength."

The honesty of her testimony was a tribute to the HELP group. They had made church a safe place in which to share truthfully that Jesus was present in the thick of emotional pain. This language was healing language. It opened the door for several people to come to HELP when they had previously been too ashamed to admit their problem. I also received several phone calls from people whose children suffered with bipolar disorder and who were grateful that we had addressed mental illness in the services.

People come from all over to an annual conference sponsored by the HELP ministry to discuss the importance of community and to learn how to incorporate those with mental illnesses into the life of the church. These people faithfully show up for one another week after week, year after year. They remember birthdays, they celebrate small victories, they don't hold back on congratulating one another. People who support those with mental illnesses are also included in the fellowship. It helps these capers to hear what supporters go through and vice versa. Open communication like this has been pivotal in facilitating trust and stamping out stigma.

The HELP group knows that avoidance is a pattern that can grow like a malignancy. The more you avoid, the less and less you see, and problems create more problems when they are not addressed. Larger and thicker blinders are necessary to continue the avoidance pattern. For instance, many people tell me they are holding their marriage together for the sake of the children, because the Bible tells them to do it. But they also confide that there is no marriage to speak of; there is nothing that makes living with their spouse joyful, uplifting or supportive. For years they have tried to "make it work" and have avoided marital counseling. They have been too ashamed to share their marital issues with friends so that they can receive prayer and support. They would rather go it alone. Now, I am a marriage proponent. I am for doing everything in your power to work out your relationship. Tim and I are living proof that if you hang on by the skin of your teeth, you can indeed work it out. We had to rebuild from scratch, and we are a different couple than we were twelve years ago. However, sometimes people would rather hang on to the shambles, walk on loose floorboards, step over rusty nails and tape over shattered windows than get out the scaffolding to rebuild.

Sometimes I try to wake folks up by saying, "So you're a hypocrite then?"

"What do you mean?" they respond, taken aback.

"Well, you're preserving the external show when internally there is nothing there. Jesus called hypocrites whitewashed tombs."

"But God hates divorce."

"Precisely," I will say. "God hates it when love goes stale, our hearts are broken by each other and promises go by the wayside. It sounds to me like you are already divorced in spirit. No sharing. No love. No intimacy. God looks on the heart. A divorce is just a piece of paper that states what often is already true."

"But the Bible says I'm supposed to submit," many women will say.

"The Bible also says that your husband is supposed to love you the way Christ loved the church," I answer (see Ephesians 5:22-28). "How did Christ love his people? He suffered and died. He told them how much he loved them, he forgave them when they messed up, he encouraged them, he wanted them with him, and he endorsed them as friends and ambassadors. It's easy to give yourself over to someone who loves you that much because he is giving himself to you in turn. This is a love relationship - the essence of marriage. I suggest that if you don't want this marriage to end in divorce - on paper, even though it seems you're already living it - that you get help. Work it through. Hammer it out. Get real, and get going."

THE LANGUAGE OF RATIONALIZATION
If we can think about a situation in a way that helps us wrap
our mind around it, it can definitely be helpful. But when our
thinking becomes a way to distance ourselves from our feelings,
we need to pause and take stock of our internal state.

"I've lost everything," someone recently confided in me. "My
house, my family, my job--gone. But God wanted it this way, so
that's it. All my days were planned ahead of time, the Scripture
says. I've just got to realize that God's will must be done."

Well, this is all too slick and too quick; it's like wallpapering
a room when the plaster is crumbling underneath. Slap on a
Scripture! Slap on a happy face! Presto-the room is done. The
building is falling apart, but it sure looks pretty. God conve-
niently gets blamed for a lot of things that are not his will at all.
Rationalizing is a process where we come up with reasons that
justify actions or consequences that are often the cause of our
own poor choices. God is an easy target. If we can blame God
rather than making clear distinctions and perhaps some difficult
decisions we can stay "stuck in the muck" of our own inertia-our
hamster-wheel process. Rationalizing also distances us from our
emotions and from an honest relationship with others and with
God.

CONCLUSION
This chapter has illustrated a few ways our patterns of thinking
encourage unproductive suffering on the hamster-wheel. This
isn't intentional or even a conscious choice for many of us, but
something needs to change if we're going to get off the hamster-wheel and onto the potter's wheel. If we're struggling with
our marriage relationship, we can notice the ways we have previously avoided our problem. Change starts when we get honest.
We call the dry bones what they really are. Say it like it is! Dry
bones have been known to rise again. This is far more hopeful,

trusting and faith-filled than denying, minimizing, spiritualizing or rationalizing our issues.

Language–the words we use–are vitally important. Jesus, the living Word, was full of grace and truth. Truth includes the pain of this world—combined with grace that assures us that the reality of resurrection life is bigger than the worst that evil can do. Grace and truth belong together. Without truth-honesty with ourselves, others and God-we will lapse into one form or another of the hamster-wheel language described in this chapter. We will find ourselves going nowhere, unable to articulate or come to terms with our own brokenness and need for God. Without grace, however, honesty gets us nowhere, except to perpetuate human despair. Grace enters in through the words of Jesus that bring forgiveness and the promised Holy Spirit to us—and the cry for this forgiveness comes to us from, the depths of Jesus' pain on a cross. These words promise us a resurrection morning, the healing of our brokenness and a chance to stop running in circles.

If you are ready to gently set aside some of your old ways of thinking, seeing, feeling and doing, then our next chapter is going to guide you in another next right step. (Remember, at this stage, we don't have to know how to think, see, feel and do differently; we are simply saying, we're ready to consider other options.)

Chapter 7

Making Decisions That Support Healing

Teresa McBean

We have spent several chapters unpacking why our spirituality and our daily life decisions are sometimes at odds with each other. As Kim pointed out previously, some of our false strategies and miscues on this journey of faith have actually served as protection. Denial can keep us safe as a child, when we lack the resources or the capacity to get free from a difficult family situation. But our strategies make for a poor life partner. Eventually, as we grow and mature, we are presented with opportunities to make healing choices and different decisions than we made when we had fewer tools or no support.

THE THIRD STEP

Kim spent an entire chapter talking about various components of false spirituality, and urged us to consider another, new way of faith. This is the intent of the first three steps of the 12-step model. First, we have to admit we need help. Next, we acknowledge that there is a God, and guess what? We didn't get that job! After these first two steps, we move on to the third step (We made a decision to turn our life and will over to the care of God.) This requires that we make a decision to trust in a God who promises all this and more:

> God knows what He's doing.
> God has a plan for your life.
> God promises never to abandon you.
> God promises to provide a future for you.
> God's future is hopeful. It is the abundant life.

These promises have a condition attached to them. This is our part. We must call out to God. He promises to listen. I know that many of us may have a history that teaches us that others do not listen when we call out. But God listens whether others do or not.

I once believed that I would never find God. I thought he was for others but not for me. I was wrong. Here's the thing, though. I read this verse, and I did it, but I can't say that I had any expectations. The world had taught me that with few expectations come fewer disappointments. But I decided to try it. I simply sought God. I followed hard after God. I did it because I couldn't see any other options. I did it whether I was in the mood or not. I did it when it didn't make sense. I often did it poorly. Fortunately, this decision is not asking us to "get it right" or work harder. It's simply inviting us to face toward God and decide to give God a chance. Sound cheeky? Maybe, but I have experienced God as thoroughly secure—willing to embrace me—even in my cheekiness.

Please offer yourself the gift of patience. The loss of hope, the feelings of helplessness, the belief that nothing will ever change—none of these false beliefs formed in an instant. We get worn down just as even the hardest stone is eventually worn down with the slow and steady dripping of water. In this step we aren't trying to figure out our theology or our denominational loyalties. We aren't committing to church membership or strict adherence to a set of religious rules. We're just crying out. We're saying: "Hey, there is a God" (even though I am not sure what he's all about). We are saying: "I am not God, and I'm going to trust that Creator God knows more about how my life works than I have been able to figure out independently on my own power." That's it. It's simple, but not easy.

I don't know a verb tense that appropriately captures the on going nature of this decision to believe and then trust.

Once I was baptizing a man who chose to reveal his decision publicly through baptism. This was a baptism by immersion—the way Jesus was baptized. First, he leaned back into the water.

Once submerged, I helped lift him back out of the water, and up he arose! Pushing hair and water out of his face and shaking off the water like a shaggy dog, he peered at me and said, "Wow! I feel different. This was a good decision." I felt a little twinge of concern because the act of baptism is not magic. But a good decision is still a good decision.

On July 15, 1978, I married my husband. The entire ceremony lasted no longer than a good baptism. Each day, however, I recommit to the decision made during our marriage ceremony. The ceremony is not what keeps us married. We're married because we make a decision daily to be committed to each other. The initial decision is vital, but the relationship must also be continual. Prior to making a third-step decision, all of us experience the ebb and flow of emotional attachment to our past hurts, habits, and hang-ups. A decision frees us from the tyranny of these emotions.

Consider this from Ephesians: "Then we will no longer be infants, tossed back and forth by the waves, and blown here and there by every wind of teaching and by the cunning and craftiness of men in their deceitful scheming" (Ephesians 4:14 NIV).

This passage goes on to say that the outcome of a third-step decision is growth. James 1:6 puts it this way: "But when he asks, he must believe and not doubt; because he who doubts is like a wave of the sea, blown and tossed by the wind." Don't you want the tossing about to stop?

It is a beautiful sight to behold—the turning over of a life and will to the care of God. But there is often more process to it than most of us would care to admit.

As my mother-in-law aged, her health required that she start turning things over. First, she had to give up her condo with the steep stairs. Eventually she moved into a wonderful community designed for people "of a certain age." It was a fight to the finish for her to acknowledge it was time to turn in her keys and stop driving. But her humility brought many of us greater peace and offered us the gift of a practical life lesson with faith implications. As I watched her humble her image of "self" (strong, independent, woman of God) to the aging process, what emerged was a woman of true dignity. She knew her body was made of dust, but never was she more beautiful than in the last days of her life. Although she needed to trust others with her care, the by-product was a rich awareness of how much she was loved. I imagine it felt scary to her to trust like this, but this is the kind of attitude toward God to which faith calls us. It is as we turn things over that we discover how much God loves us.

WE DON'T NEED PERFECT UNDERSTANDING TO MAKE A DECISION

There is a phrase in the third step, "as we understood him," that used to confuse me. I thought it meant that we could just make up a god that pleased us. That's not what this means. This phrase is expressing the very heart of the 12 steps: process. The only way we can relate to God is at the level at which we understand God. Through the process of working the 12 steps, our understanding will grow. But here's the really cool thing: God patiently accepts us wherever we are in the process just as he initially accepted Gideon. (See Judges 6 – 8 to read my favorite biblical illustration of this concept.) God accepted Gideon just where he was in his development, but didn't leave him stuck. He challenged, encouraged, and provided for Gideon to move from where he was to where God intended for him to be: Gideon the mighty warrior. I won't spoil the story for you, but I encourage you to go read it for yourself. It's awesome. God is not a theory or idea or concept or notion. God is real. And God wants a personal relationship with us.

My husband is slightly colorblind. Sometimes he wants to believe that a particular favorite shirt is navy blue. It is not. It is black. No amount of his understanding it to be blue will make it blue. The shirt is black. After lots of years of failing to trust my color sense over his own defective color vision, time has taught him to trust me. If he shows up for breakfast in a mismatched outfit, he is willing to go up and try again if I mention the color snafu. If you feel, as I once did, that you will never understand this God stuff or if you have trouble believing that your vision of who God is might be impaired, fear not. God gives his wisdom freely to us, without finding fault. (See James 1.) Trusting can grow over time.

I was in a meeting room recently, and a young woman fresh out of her third rehab facility said the most profound thing. She said, "The 12 steps are a simple program for complicated people." The third step is choosing to simplify. It's firing ourselves from running our own lives and asking God to get down here and save us. This is not an easy process. It invites us to become more conscious of how our beliefs and our behaviors do (or do not) "match up." We can understand from Kim's story why she needed to do this kind of work, and as we study this material, perhaps we will also catch a vision for why we need to follow her lead.

Chapter 8

The Blame Game

Kim Engelmann

People in AA have a special phrase for the way we revert to thought patterns that keep us trapped on the hamster wheel: they call it "stinking thinking." Two patterns of stinking thinking seem particularly operative in Christian culture. (If the Christian culture isn't the world that you are familiar with, that's okay. Perhaps as you read this chapter, you can think about how these concepts have operated within the culture where you live.) Both have to do with blame and judgment rather than grace and truth.

RIGID THINKING

Once couples have children, they often return to the church even if they don't have a personal faith of their own. They do this because they want their children to be "good people" and learn moral values. They want their kids to know what's right and wrong. And there's nothing wrong with that. It's a good thing to want children to be trained properly.

But going to church just for the sake of moral values is limited in scope and dimension, and it won't last. It's like expecting cut flowers to look nice longer than a week or two. Cut off from the source of life—the God who wants us to live our lives out of love for him—moral values wither and die. Ultimately, worthwhile values must spring out of our love for Jesus. Gradually, as a result of spending time with him, we begin to live as he did. Not because we're trying hard but because the Holy Spirit produces the fruit of God in us. This process pulls the Christian life out of the realm of dos and don'ts and into the reality of a love relationship with God that is intricately connected to everyday life.

A harsh "moral values" mindset is an example of the kind of

thinking that sacrifices people to principle. I find that people use rigid thinking as a way to make complicated problems simple. Many people who are extremely rigid in how they come across have huge internal struggles with immoral thoughts and actions. They appeal to a black-and-white model of thought to try to keep themselves in line with what they believe God wants.

However, this kind of simplistic thinking doesn't translate effectively to the complexity of life and the depth of what it means to be a human being. The truth is that Jesus lived in the gray. He loved to hang in the murky backwater of life with the outcasts and sinners. He did ascribe to certain standards of behavior, which we would find life-giving to ascribe to as well. But in the gray of life, we in our limited earthly scope can be hard-pressed to tell which people are "good" and which are "bad."

Do we have a spiritual telescope that can look into the hearts of everyone and categorize them like species of ants? This one goes in the righteous pile. This one gets damned. This one has done some awful things but says she's sorry, so she's okay. This one isn't sorry but ought to be, so he gets scratched off the list. Obviously there are no such definitive distinctions. Do we even know when someone accepts Christ whether he or she has done it from the heart? We can hope that it is so, but we never know for sure.

"Not everyone who says to me, 'Lord, Lord': will enter the kingdom of heaven," Jesus told the people (Matthew 7:21). We aren't the ones commissioned to separate the sheep from the goats. That's what God does, and his mercy is beyond our comprehension. It isn't our position to figure it out. Our rigid structures, inflexible critiques and strict formulas cannot hope to match up with the intricacies of human life. Only God, who sees the heart, is judge. Thank God it's God! "We have not been given the authority to judge," Pentecostal minister David du Plessis said years ago. "We have only been given the authority to forgive."

This is where our right-and-wrong abstractions butt heads with specific individuals and circumstances—with real life. If Jesus had been worried about the moral values of his time he never would have associated with tax collectors and sinners. He never would have healed non-Jews or saved a prostitute's life when the law dictated that she be destroyed. Jesus said, "What I speak ... I speak just as the Father has told me" (John 12:50). He said nothing about moral values--ever. He said everything about his relationship with God.

PROJECTIVE THINKING

When you go to a cinema, the movie projector takes what is inside it and projects it out onto the screen. You hardly think about the mechanism behind you. Rather, your focus is elsewhere. This is what happens in relational projection as well.

Projection is essentially putting onto another person or institution all the bad things (or good things) that we don't want to acknowledge as our own. Often the church is a target for projection when people are angry at God about something difficult in their lives. I can't count the number of times someone has come to me and said, "This church doesn't care. No one understands or makes any attempt to reach out to me. I'm not going to come anymore. This place is a poor representation of the body of Christ."

I used to nod and say, "I'm sorry to hear that" and go on with my day with a little chip on my shoulder. Now I begin to ask questions about the reported experiences. I listen as they explain how they have felt misunderstood or abandoned. The list is sometimes long, but at the core is usually a recent experience of significant loss or trauma. I wonder if what they really want to say is, "I hate God." They are enraged that he has allowed pain and heartache to invade their lives, and the church is an easier target for anger than God. You can see it. You can pound on its walls. You can yell at its people. You can stop coming. So there!

Usually, if people have, in actuality, been well cared for and loved by the church, they will leave for six months to a year and then return. But sometimes people who project their bad feelings onto churches will church shop all their lives. They never seem to be able to settle in and find rest within a community of faith. As AA says, "Wherever you go, there you are." This isn't really about running from church (or marriages or AA home groups or miserable work environments); it's about running from ourselves.

Churches can breed projection, especially when they emphasize that "we are righteous" and "they are sinful." If I am "righteous," then all my problems can be attributed to society's ills, to the riffraff who hang out by the corner liquor store, to misguided laws, to bad people, to poor leadership, and to my Aunt Betty who never shaves her legs.

Within the church community, spiritual rigidity and projection can reinforce defenses that inhibit rather than encourage emotional healing. When we quote our words as God's words, we use language as a lacquer to paint over deep-rooted problems. These problems will not go away unless they are dealt with directly and genuinely. It would be a good discipline to strip ourselves of Christian lingo and talk like the rest of the world occasionally to see if there's any meaning under our reflexive sayings. "Praise the Lord" might be better received by non-Christians (and me, too, actually) if we simply said, "Am I ever grateful that I can live this day in God's presence." If this is what we really mean, then we can say it. We don't need to sugarcoat it or use religious words to distance ourselves from what's really going on inside— good or bad.

Authenticity in speech and action from Christians would come as a healing balm to many who stand outside the church, perceiving it to be an irrelevant group of people who are perpetually nice but generally ineffective when it comes to real-life issues. Much of this negativity toward church could be transformed if we would trust God and one another enough to lay on the line exactly what we think and feel. Good therapy and working through the 12-step process can help us know what we think and feel if we are having trouble figuring it out. Then perhaps we can learn to use the words of Scripture effectively and with integrity, not as a means to perpetuate our defenses. It has been a revelation to me that the more vulnerable I am in the pulpit - the more I get rid of spiritual pomposity and evangelical lingo and simply share my life experience including my foibles and failures-the more people resonate. When I express my brokenness, my uncertainty about what God is doing, or on the other hand my joy in the love of Jesus, people soak it up like dry sponges. They weep, they shake my hand, they want to talk more, they say, "Thank you!" All I have done is share honestly. It's that simple.

I am going to say it again: Stating the problem is the first step (Remember the first step, the one where we admit that our life is unmanageable and we are powerless to change it?) toward healing. In keeping ourselves honest and trusting God enough to be genuine before him and others, we can grow together as wounded but fellow travelers, all in need of God's love. The language of Jesus was always honest and non-defensive. It was meant to lift burdens, not lay them on heavier. The language of Jesus opened the way for us to enter the kingdom. It brought us freedom from isolation, from ourselves, from others, and from God.

On the cross Jesus demonstrated ultimate vulnerability while revealing to us the utter despair of our own condition. When he appeared to the disciples as resurrected Lord, he wasn't ashamed of his wounds. He was resurrected with the scars still in his hands, and he showed them to his closest friends.

In Jesus' own body he joined pain, wounds, brokenness, and the memory of horrific brutality with resurrection life and power. This is our story as Christians: in this world we live pain and resurrection together. Classically this has been called "the already and the not yet." The already is the resurrection joy of the Holy Spirit forming us, teaching us and alive in us. The not yet is the scars we bear, the brokenness and weakness in us, the areas where we are vulnerable and terribly human.

If hell on earth is being stabbed over and over with the same wound as we cycle through old patterns, heaven on earth must be the process of acknowledging our wounds as Jesus did, knowing where they are and not being afraid to show them to the world. The wounds of Jesus were the proof Thomas needed to believe in the resurrection.

If we are honest and genuine, we are not afraid to show our wounds. "To be alive is to be broken," states Brennan Manning in *The Ragamuffin Gospel*. We don't need a false spiritual language to coat over what is really going on. We don't need spiritual words to lacquer over the pain, scars and deep wounds that life inevitably brings. Rather, we can say, "Here, look! This should have killed me--this battle wound right here, and here and here. These are my scars. Take a good look at where I am imperfect and even downright disgusting. It is an amazing thing that I live, but I do! You can be just as amazed as I am at the goodness of God. Because Jesus lives and has set me free, so I live and am free. The very pain that ought to have destroyed me has actually made me stronger and more alive. And I don't blame you for these wounds. You are forgiven!"

One of the gifts of the twelve steps is the opportunity to work on, and through, our confusions about possible prior spiritual abuse, past wounding (both the wounds we have received and those we have inflicted), and the many strategies we've used to protect ourselves. Kim mentioned these in past chapters. They include: denial, minimization, reactionary living, avoidance, rationalization, rigid thinking, projective thinking, etc. Although these different ways of coping may have helped us at some point in our lives, when we commit to hopping off the hamster's wheel and onto the Potter's wheel, we're going to examine our previous ways of thinking, feeling, doing, and "seeing" life. Each of us has a certain way of "seeing." And although this is difficult to hear, it's nevertheless true: we might be better served by inviting others to help us expand and clear our vision. Maybe we've been right and we've seen accurately. But recovery work invites us to see beyond the facts of right versus wrong and consider the possibility that as we awaken to a new perspective on God, ourselves and even other people – we may discover an inspired "new way" of seeing.

In the next chapter, we are going to consider how we might begin to examine our past life (which is painful at times), but not for the purpose of navel gazing and using old strategies to cope with this process. Instead, we're going to take our past decision to turn our life over to the care of God, and apply it by actually making an inventory of our life experiences. Some people like to skip this step – and I understand the temptation. But for those of us who have worked this step, we want you to know how healing this honest moral inventory can be for those who do it. In AA they say, "Nothing changes if nothing changes." Step four helps us start to figure out how awesome change can be for those who have chosen to do so within a framework of trusting God.

Chapter 9

Self-examination, a Necessary Next Step

Teresa McBean

In the previous chapter, Kim quoted from Brennan Manning's work *The Ragamuffin Gospel*. It's so important that I want to repeat it. "To be alive is to be broken." Most of us are nodding in collective agreement over this statement, but do we know what to do with our brokenness? Is our only option returning again and again to our story of brokenness, hoping that somehow God will magically remove our suffering? Or, for some of us, believing in all that Jesus was about, do we feel like we cannot admit to anyone that our wounds often feel raw and unhealed? Kim gave several examples of distorted ways we think (rigid and projective), reminding us that we bring this habitual way of thinking with us when we come to church. Or to an AA meeting. We take our way of thinking, seeing, doing and feeling with us everywhere we go! Sometimes, the only common denominator in all our old and familiar ways of suffering is….us.

IMPORTANT NEXT RIGHT STEPS

This is the beauty of the process that is the 12 steps. It provides a pathway to travel that allows us not only to believe in God and to turn our lives over to him, but to know what to do with our sufferings as well. The fourth step requires courage. It prepares us for the next stage of the process: making peace with ourselves. I find that self-objectivity is a difficult task. It feels burdensome at times. But learning how to see myself accurately enables me to understand how others see me. Why is this so crucial for our healing? From the beginning of time God had us in mind and created us as relational beings. We weren't meant to live in isolation or constant conflict. In Genesis, we find that the first thing God said was "not good" in his created kingdom was that man was alone.

In the New Testament, a crowd of people asked Jesus what is the most important commandment. He gave them two answers: love God, and love others as you love yourself. Isn't that fascinating? He didn't command them to achieve world peace, end poverty, or fight for the rights of the underprivileged. He said "love." Loving God, self, and others is all about relationships. I believe that world peace, the cessation of poverty, and fighting for the rights of the underprivileged are all awesome passions to pursue. We know, though, that they stem from an inspired way of seeing. They are our response to love. Jesus knew that if we would love God, self, and others we would be ready, willing, and able to fight for any cause God set before us.

We can't live out the two most important commandments if we are incapable of living in relationship with others. First, we can't love others if we have not made peace with ourselves. Second, we will struggle to live lovingly with others if we do not understand how others perceive us.

One day I was walking out of a store, and my son evidently watched me trudge across the parking lot. When I climbed in the car, he asked:

"Mom, are you okay?"

"Yes, I'm fine. Why do you ask?"

"Your face looked kind of stressed."

"It did? Thanks for telling me. I was just thinking. My face wasn't matching my insides because my insides are really happy."

He continued, "You know, my friends say that I'm going to have a permanent wrinkle across my face because I walk around looking stressed." He said this with that tone we use when we're in the middle of an insight.

"Huh," I said. "I guess that's why I often ask you if you're stressed when I pick you up from school. I wonder if you and I share that trait. When we're thinking, I wonder if other people see us and think we're stressed out."

"I asked my friends, 'What do you want me to do, look like this?'" He made an exaggerated happy face that could not possibly be considered an upgrade in facial expressions. I laughed. He's a funny guy.

"I don't know what the solution is, but you and I have both learned something about ourselves today. If our facial expressions don't match how we feel in our hearts, we will confuse other people. I guess we both need to work on making our outsides and insides match."

"I guess." He was finished with this conversation. I realize what a valuable lesson I learned, thanks to my son. These kinds of lessons and more await us as we enter into the fourth-step process.

I often think of the Old Testament character, Gideon, when I think about the fourth step. Gideon was a guy willing to do a fourth step. Prior to his remarkable encounter with his true God-created self, he was hiding out in a cave. He believed himself to be the runt of his litter—the least in his clan—born to a clan that was the least of all clans. But God saw him differently:

"...The Lord is with you, mighty warrior." (Judges 6:12 NIV)

Gideon didn't believe this message from the Lord, but he went on to do a partial fourth step. He named his shortcomings, and I suppose he expected the angel to agree. I wonder if he just thought the angel would say, "Yeah, you're right, dude. Sorry to bug you." Did he then expect the angel to leave him there, hiding in his cave of desperation? You may want to read Judges 6 and see what happens to Gideon, but in case you don't read it, I'll tell you that he becomes the mighty warrior he was created to be. It wasn't easy, but God gently guided him through his defects and revealed to Gideon his potential.

THE FOURTH STEP

The fourth step (We made a searching and fearless moral inventory of ourselves.) is challenging. What do we mean when we talk about taking a moral inventory? "A moral inventory is a list of our weaknesses and our strengths. This inventory is something we prayerfully accomplish with God's help. It is for our benefit."[3]

There are many ways to do an inventory. The most important part of this process is that we actually do it. Almost everyone emphasizes the importance that an inventory be done in writing and without us stopping to evaluate our writing in the middle of the process. It is kind of like a written "life review," so don't hesitate to include remembrances from childhood. Here are some approaches that I have found to be helpful:

1) Write a list of all the people, institutions, or principles that you resent, and why. Explain how you feel these people, institutions or principles have harmed you.

2) Write a list of all your fears. Write down why you fear people, institutions, or principles and explain how your fears have harmed you.

3) Make a list of all your grudges and injuries (real or imagined). Include in this list all the harm others have done to you. Some people hesitate, thinking that theirs are grudges or injuries unworthy of being mentioned. Don't filter your inventory—just write! Complain and whine all you want. The rest of the process will put an end to this self-pity, so don't hold back now!

---

3. Friends in Recovery, *The Twelve Steps for Christians* (RPI Publishing Inc., 1994) p. 71.

4) Make a list of all the problem areas in your life. Common areas of concern are: finances, sex, marriage, work, etc.

5) Write a list of all the things you've done that have resulted in your feeling guilty. Include all the people, institutions, etc. that you have harmed. Again, don't pre-filter your list. Sometimes we have false guilt—that's guilt that really belongs to someone else. God's word teaches us that "there is no condemnation for those who are in Christ Jesus." (Romans 8:1). This step will help clarify these confusing issues.

6) List your assets. It's like doing inventory at a store. See what's there and write it down. One of the positive things that I recorded on my first inventory was how I changed my relationship with food once I knew it was unhealthy. I also considered it an asset that I was always seeking a better way to live. You have assets too, so write them down. (Sometimes it's harder to include the assets.)

7) Another recommended list is very simple: write down anything that upsets you, bothers you, bugs you, or gets under your skin. It's good to report how this makes you feel and what you believe about bothersome situations. God doesn't want our emotions managed; he wants them resolved. Mike O'Neill says: "Emotions are like visitors: they're supposed to show up, tell you something, and then they're supposed to leave."[4] If we don't resolve our emotions, then they don't leave. They hang around and become the roots of all kinds of unhealthy behaviors that ultimately require us to do more fourth step work. Consider these emotions as possibilities for things to inventory: anger, lust, greed, jealousy, laziness, paranoia, depression, anxiety, insecurity, irresponsibility, lying, pride, oversensitivity, apathy, rationalization, self-pity, gossip, ingratitude, rudeness, rigidity, judgmental attitudes, complaining, evasiveness, dishonesty, con-

---

4 Mike O'Neil, *Power to Choose* (Sonlight Publications Inc., 1992) p. 72.

trol, over-compliance, violence, and more.

As you make all these lists, it is important to do so with a spirit of self-acceptance rather than shame. Your list of wrongdoings will probably increase your awareness that you have harmed others. That will not feel good. But treating yourself badly is not the solution. The attitude of self-condemnation helps no one. It hinders the recovery process just as profoundly as failing to admit legitimate wrongdoing.

One word of caution: as you are working through this step, keep it personal and private. Step 5 will provide an opportunity to share and interact with others about what you're writing down. As you search, just write. Don't try to figure out what you're writing. Don't judge yourself or make excuses. Most of us develop reactionary patterns of behaving simply as coping strategies. No one wakes up every morning and says, "How can I mess up my life today?" Just write. Remember, all you're doing is making the inventory. Now is not the time to think ahead; just make the list. I would suggest that you write as if no one will ever look at this list.

Recently I had in a lengthy conversation with a person who had relapsed. There were a lot of reasons: life was too stressful, the boss fired him, no one would give him a ride to a meeting, nobody would lend him money to pay the rent and on and on. He was doing a pretty good job of making an inventory of other people's problems. But a fourth step is not an inventory of other people's stuff. A fourth step inventory is a personal evaluation of our own stuff. In Lamentations 3:40, we are told to examine our ways, test them, and return to the Lord. No mention is made of examining others. In 1 Corinthians 11:28, we're told to examine ourselves before we take communion. Self-examination is a spiritual practice. Self-examination is not the same as being self-focused. Living a self-focused life gets us into trouble, but self-examination helps us get clear about the kinds of changes that we need to make. Honestly, we all would like it if we could skip this step. Some of us avoid this step by pretending that we don't have anything to inventory. Some of us avoid it by being so overwhelmed with the feelings of shame and inadequacy that we just can't get started. Either response tends to make us run from the process, but step 4 is absolutely essential. It will help anyone who enters into the 12-step process break the cycle of shame-based living.

After my friend lamented his long and sad list of reasons why he just had to drink, I offered him a slightly different way to tell his story. Here's where he ended up:

"I noticed I was feeling more stress lately. I was having trouble sleeping, I was eating more junk food than I had in a long time. I was irritable too. Instead of talking to my sponsor about this, I started taking Ambien to sleep, and I spent a lot of time thinking about why people were so irritating."

"When my boss fired me, I just stormed out. I drove around thinking about what a jerk she was, and I didn't tell anyone in my family, my home group at AA, my church, or my sponsor that I had gotten fired because I felt not only angry, but pretty embarrassed, ashamed, and afraid. I worried that people would think I had relapsed."

"I sold my truck to pay the rent, and then I didn't have a ride to meetings. I was too embarrassed to tell anyone that I couldn't pay my rent, so I told everyone my truck was stolen. I couldn't really talk about not having a ride to meetings, because I really didn't want to get into why I didn't have my truck anymore."

"It's true, I really freaked out the second month when I didn't have rent money. But the thing is, I didn't tell anyone my problem. I just assumed no one would give a drunk rent money, and I can't say that I blame them. You know, when I was using before, I kind of used up all the good will of people who loved me. I made a vow to never ask for money from anyone again."

My friend had a lot going on in his head that he never shared; instead, he relapsed. Once he sat down and reframed his previously rigid, projective, rationalizing, blaming thinking within the framework of step four, he had a moment of clarity. As of this writing, my friend is ten years sober without relapse—since the day he came clean about his thinking, not just his drinking.

This is an example of a guy who moved off the hamster wheel, and onto the potter's wheel. He used the tool of the 12-step process to guide his transition. Even escaping the hamster wheel is a God thing. And it often takes the collaborative, communal effort of those who've gone before us to teach us how to step off of one wheel and climb up, onto the other, better way. Kim's going to share her experience of wheel hopping in the next chapter.

Chapter 10

What Happens When We Stop the Wheel

Kim Engelmann

I met my husband, Tim, while I was attending Barnard College in Manhattan and he was at Columbia. As undergrads we dated for two-and-a-half years, and we got married two weeks after graduation. As I write this I have just celebrated my 25th wedding anniversary But 12 years ago, no one would have predicted that a twenty-fifth anniversary was on the horizon.

I had unwittingly married an alcoholic, and though I cared deeply for him, the same cycle of unpredictability, denial and false spiritual language that had marked my family of origin was now prevalent in our home. I was reliving my past and didn't know it. I was a "co"-codependent. I knew how to dance around and care for another person. I knew how to deny problems and convince myself things weren't so bad. I had done it for years with my mother, and I had never figured out that life could be different. I was wearing blinders, focused on how to survive rather than how to live. Meanwhile life was passing me by.

Being a "co" in our marriage worked for quite a while—13 years. Things weren't wonderful, but they were better than they had been when I was growing up. I kept holding on and making things work. Then my husband's alcoholism and prescription drug abuse skyrocketed as his productivity quotas increased at work. Life morphed into a nightmare. Tim lost his job. He became a man I didn't know. With a four-month-old, a two-year-old and a four-year-old I was desperate, once again at the receiving end of crazy and unpredictable behavior. One night I did what I had never done before. I opted out of the hamster wheel.

I woke up one morning and sensed the presence of God in a

way I never had in the past. It was a directive presence with a sense of urgency about it. Perhaps Joseph experienced this same presence in his dream when the angel told him to take the infant Jesus to Egypt so he would be safe (Matthew 2:13-15). I knew very clearly that morning that the situation I was living in could not be healed by my resolve to stay in it. This clarity was a divine gift. The directive to leave was clear, firm, and something I knew I must do quickly. A day later I took the three children, put them in the car, and drove off. The next day I boarded a plane for California and went to visit a friend who had invited me to stay with her. "If you come out here," she told me, "I will help you. I will take care of you." And that's what I did.

Following God's directive did not mean the experience was easy. The next year and a half I was more lonely and exhausted than I could ever remember being. I longed for the man I loved, yet I knew I couldn't be with him. People told me to give up, to get on with my life—as if I had any clue how to do that. With three small children, I could barely make it to the grocery store. I would put one child in the cart, strap another in a carrier, and have the oldest run alongside. In an unfamiliar place with no family support, I felt like I was on an island, completely alone with no one but myself to depend on for my survival and my children's well-being. Yet there was something different about this time of suffering than in my previous experiences. Things kept happening to me that assured me of God's presence. Prayers kept being answered. Hope seemed to invade my life for no reason. Like background music that creates a mood of drama, this assurance was a source of expectation, energy and life. People would look at me with disapproval - a single mom with three small kids!

"A walking charity case," I heard someone whisper with a sidelong glance one day as I walked by. I felt like a complete loser, yet at the same time I had this deep unshakable assurance that somehow, in God's timing, all I had lost would be restored. I kept being pointed to a horizon where the sun was just about to come up. I was catching the early morning rays of hope. I was tasting it before there was anything to be hopeful about.

HEALING, ONE STEP AT A TIME

A year and a half later my husband, Tim, joined us. He had finally hit bottom and was in the beginning stages of recovery. Bit by bit, step by step, we worked our way back into each other's arms. Little by little, trust grew between us as AA, counseling, prayer and people's love helped us along. We are now a family in recovery, and we will always be in recovery. In fact, it is our story of recovery that brings many to see Tim in his clinical psychology practice. They want someone "real," they say, who has been through it and come out on the other side. Tim and I have learned who we are, we have put first things first, we have hung on to one another for love's sake, and we have learned and continue to learn how to love. Our marriage is better than it has ever been, and as one that is refined in the furnace, so we have been changed.

Not that we don't still have our struggles, discouragements and differences. Our marriage is human, and it will never be perfect. But we have changed in such a way that we are not repeating old patterns of chaos and confusion. Getting off the hamster wheel was painful and difficult and exhausting – but so worth it! Both of us have gone to hell and back for the relationship that we are now able to enjoy. Someone once described us as Lazarus come back from the dead.

At times, Tim and I look at each other and just laugh. We weren't supposed to make it. We weren't supposed to hope. The odds were stacked against us. So we laugh because we see how good God is after everything has gone stale and life seems to have gone down the drain. In a cold, stone tomb resurrection happens. The sun does rise, the Lord is faithful, and people who get off the hamster wheel can be transformed.

During the days of our reconciliation, Tim and I realized that we couldn't simply build onto the precarious structure of our past relationship, adding another balcony to a toppling building with a poor foundation. What we had to do was dismantle and start over; knock down the old and build from the ground up, bit by bit, creating something healthy, secure, and entirely new.

The knocking down part took place during our separation. The real challenge was the rebuilding and dismantling of old patterns, finding new ways of relating. In order to do this we had to learn who we were as individuals first; only then could we come together as partners and lovers in a new way, committed and surrendered to God. It was not easy. I emphasize this because many people believe that when you are in God's will, everything happens without pain. But Scripture says, "Beloved, do not be surprised at the fiery ordeal that is taking place among you to test you, as though something strange were happening to you" (1 Peter 4:12). For my husband and me, losing old habits and discovering new ways to listen and learn from each other took patience, persistence and prayer. The counseling we went through was brutal. I often wanted to give up. And yet the hard work, the pain and the ongoing challenge brought us somewhere. This kind of process is what I call potter's wheel suffering.

The potter's wheel is different from the hamster wheel because it is redemptive. You get off it in a different shape than when you got on. It produces transformation. And yet the process of being molded is not necessarily pleasant. Potters slam the clay around a lot at the beginning. This hammering and pounding realigns molecules so that the clay can become stronger and hold up as the potter continues to work with it. If the clay could talk, it would probably tell the potter that it didn't like being slammed around one bit. But in that awkward lump the potter sees the future result, and he continues to pound and mold with hope and expectation. The clay does not move the wheel at its own pace and for its own purposes the way the hamster does. Rather, the potter drives the wheel as he sees fit. The clay never finds itself alone on the wheel. The potter's hand is in the mix and shapes the whole process, seeing the end from the beginning.

Potter's-wheel imagery is used both in the Old Testament (Isaiah 29: 16; 45:9; Jeremiah 18:6) and the New (Romans 9:21), always with God as the potter. This language is used to emphasize not only God's sovereignty but his ability to right a wrong and purify a wayward nation, even if it means pain.

> Does the clay say to the one who fashions it, "What are you making"? or "Your work has no handles"? (Isaiah 45:9)

My growth has meant pain. The potter's wheel has involved a great deal of tears, prayer, and psychotherapy, along with the hard work of forgiveness and a deep resolve to endure so that my shattered life could be "reset" and I could heal completely. People in 12-step programs say, "It works if you work it." I don't think it is a coincidence that the word "work" appears twice.

Before I got off the hamster wheel, l always felt a disconnect when I read about Jesus coming to give us "abundant life" so that "our joy might be made complete." I was supposed to live a certain way, but I couldn't seem to actualize it. I was running around and around but not going anywhere. Not changing. Not flourishing. Just surviving. I was working very hard - my brow was wet, my breathing heavy - but I always got off right where I got on. Isaiah puts it like this:

> Why do you spend your money
> for that which is not bread,
> and your labor
> for that which does not satisfy?
> Listen carefully to me, and eat" what is good,
> and delight yourselves in rich food.
> Incline your ear, and come to me;
> listen, so that you may live. (Isaiah 55:2-3)

Scripture is full of these claims, that though we live in a world full of agony and injustice, God's grace, mercy, and compassion are more powerful than the deepest, darkest pit. When we do it God's way (which always involves the potter's wheel at some point), our souls come alive. We are not destroyed; rather we belong to the Author of Life and have a purpose and call that is larger than life. The abundant life is an awareness that I am caught up and involved in something bigger than myself, and this something is a Someone who is my liberator and friend.

"In him we live and move and have our being" (Acts 17:28).

This brings a joy, a hope, a renewal that is larger than our circumstances. The presence of Jesus assures us that we are on the right wheel.

People can experience similar life circumstances and reach very different outcomes depending on what wheel they're on. Take the example of an extramarital affair, either sexual or emotional. I remember one woman who told me that she was left alone night after night while her husband talked on the phone with a female colleague whom he was trying to "help." The wife kept trying to get her husband's attention and lure him back. Her suffering and loneliness were profound, but they were of the hamster-wheel variety. This wasn't the first time the husband had become overly involved in helping attractive females. The pattern was not recognized, and no intervention was made - outside of the wife continuing to believe that she, on her own steam, could and would gain back her husband's love and attention. The couple did not seek marital therapy, join a support group or consider working a "program" different from their historical pattern of suffering. Eventually the marriage disintegrated.

In a similar situation, a husband had an ongoing sexual affair but returned to his wife, deeply remorseful, after six months. The couple sought marital therapy and worked on the hard challenge of forgiveness. It was a painful process, but the result, years later, is a solid marriage and a happy family. Through the pain, this couple realized what mattered most. They got off the hamster wheel, got on the potter's wheel and ended up a differ-ent shape—a far better shape—than when they got on. Both sit-uations were extremely painful, but the latter involved remorse, forgiveness, reaching out, getting help and a strong commitment to change on the part of both husband and wife.

Recently it occurred to me, after I had sat through several pastoral counseling sessions that were like a series of hamster wheels, one after the other, that when cyclical patterns become the norm, they form—if you will allow me another rodent-relat-ed metaphor—a maze with no exit. We might be on a path that looks like it's leading somewhere, but we find ourselves retrac-ing our steps time after time. There is no way out unless we can somehow rise up from the maze vertically. Aha! An additional dimension is exactly what is needed. With it we can lift out of the maze entirely and be set down on a clean white expanse where we are no longer constrained by old patterns. We can actually go somewhere and experience new things! Realiza-tion of the need to move vertically happens once we admit that there is no horizontal exit.

In order to move vertically, we must be willing to reach out for another person's perspective. We have to realize that we're wear-ing ourselves out on a problem that has no solution from within the maze. For instance, if I had not left the chaos of my home and reached for outside help, I don't believe we would have recovered as a family. Had Tim not reached up from the maze of his addiction and sought help after he hit bottom, he would have destroyed himself. Had my mother been able to reach out and get professional guidance, our lives would have been far health-ier.

God's calling for each individual, which he longs to fulfill in us, can't be realized if we're following a pattern of futility. Old patterns do not bring change, though the temptation is to keep thinking they will.

The devil prowls around, looking for someone to devour"
(1 Peter 5:8).

"The thief comes only to steal
and kill and destroy.
I came that they may have life,
and have it abundantly"
(John 10:10).

We are devoured when we run in circles. Our lives are stolen
from us, and our hopes and dreams are killed off slowly over
time. Old, tired patterns of futility will make us old and tired
too.

Christ was all about breaking up old patterns. Do you remember to whom he first appeared after his resurrection? It was to
women! In ancient times, women were considered the worst
witnesses. Their testimony wouldn't even hold up in court. Many
women could not leave the house or courtyard without a man's
permission. They were meant to stay passive and compliant,
under the authority of father or husband. This was the old pattern—the norm. Yet Jesus taught something different. He taught
women about trust and action. Trusting God, they were to move
out in faith and become something new. They were to go and be
his witnesses.

Moments before, the women had thought there was no way out
of their predicament. Jesus was dead. His body was gone. Suddenly they turned around and everything they had thought was
hopeless was gloriously full of life and wonder. The resurrection
had put them in a new place and reshaped their perspective. The
potter's wheel of the cross where they had wept led to a resurrection morning in which they were liberated.

"You're it," Jesus declared. "You are my witnesses." It was up to
them to respond.

Jesus asked the woman at the well to go and get her husband.

He told the woman who was healed of the flow of blood to go in peace. He told the woman accused of adultery to go and sin no more. The word is go. Now that you have encountered me, he says, go and perpetrate life, not death. Jesus never issues a call to passivity-a mandate to retrace old patterns. He calls us to act on the reality that we are honored and loved, "Go in my name!" is a command that conveys tremendous worth. We go in the name of Jesus like ambassadors of a country or representatives of royalty. The call to pull ourselves out of old paths that foster oppression and fear and begin to represent the grace and mercy of Jesus is a call that sets us free.

Freedom from isolation, self-absorption, and fear often comes from doing time on the potter's wheel. In The Gifts of the Jews, Thomas Cahill writes that the Jewish people were the one ancient race that believed history was more than a cyclical process of life and death, endlessly repeating itself for no purpose, which was what the pagans believed at the time. The Jews believed that there was divine meaning in the flow of events and processes through time. They believed that God was involved and had a plan.

To find the plan God has for us, to see the significance of our existence, we must look at our lives honestly. In Henri Nouwen's classic work, *Can You Drink the Cup?* he tells his readers that before we drink the cup, we must hold it:

> Holding the cup of life means looking critically at what we are living. This requires great courage, because when we start looking, we might be terrified by what we see. Questions may arise that we don't know how to answer. Doubts may come up about things we thought we were sure about. Fear may emerge from unexpected places. We are tempted to say: "Let's just live life. All this thinking about it only makes things harder." Still, we intuitively know that without looking at life critically we lose our vision and our direction. When we drink the cup without holding it first, we may simply get drunk and wander around

aimlessly. Holding the cup of life is a hard discipline...
We need ... to put both of our hands around the cup and
ask ourselves, "What am I given to drink? What is in my
cup? Is it safe to drink? Is it good for me? Will it bring me
health?"

Potter's-wheel formation is what Nouwen is talking about when
he says it is a hard discipline to hold the cup of life. The familiar
ways of doing things, even if they are unhealthy or destructive,
feel safe if we don't look too closely. Moving from the hamster's
wheel to the potter's wheel can be scary. We might be called to
something unfamiliar and challenging. We know there will be
a period of formation and change. Looking critically at our life
reveals things we'd rather not see, and we can easily avoid honest
reflection with our current pace of life. I often wonder if we keep
the hamster wheel going at such a dizzying speed not out of
necessity but because we are unwilling to hold our cup and look
at who we have become. This frenetic cycling keeps us off the
potter's wheel and safe from the pain of formation. But it also
keeps us in bondage and from being flexible in God's hand.

A WAY OF ESCAPE

I spoke at a recent women's retreat, and a potter actually molded
a pot on a wheel next to me as I spoke about the importance
of formation. And Sharon was no amateur. Her work had been
featured in upscale magazines and her services contracted out
by wealthy homeowners who wanted specialized pieces in one
case a whole wall of sculptured art.

However, despite Sharon's talent and creativity, standing on the
platform that day was not easy for her. In molding a beautiful
pot from an awkward piece of clay, she herself was taking a great
risk. She had told me that she was very afraid to stand in front
of people, and she was worried that the pot wouldn't come out
right. I wanted to ask her some spontaneous questions about the
process of working with clay, and she was concerned that she
wouldn't have the right answers. She shared with me that she
had spent the last two years caring for her critically ill daughter

who had cancer. The care had been intense and grueling, and the daily grind had isolated and drained her. Her daughter was better now, but she herself was still recovering from the ordeal. She was far more comfortable doing pottery at home - not with large groups of people watching. In fact, she had never done this before. Working alone was more familiar and felt much safer.

"But I want to try," she said. "Despite all my nervousness, I want to reach out by sharing myself in this way. If the pot doesn't work out while you're talking, then I'll simply make another one. And if I don't know the answer to a question, I will just say 'I don't know.' This is a place where I need to grow. I need community and I want to go for it."

Here was a woman who was holding the cup of her life, examining it critically and making a conscious choice to move into an unfamiliar area so she could be shaped in a new way. It was scary; it was a challenge, but Sharon did it anyway.

It was a wonderful experience, both for me and for her. When we presented in front of the group, she answered my questions so easily that we let some people in the audience take the microphone and ask questions as well.

Not only was Sharon providing a visual illustration of what I was talking about that evening, but the movement from hamster wheel to potter's wheel was happening in her own life in the context of a loving community of faith. The praise and affirmation from the group after she finished was profound. This woman, who had gone through so much alone, was surrounded by people who wanted to know her better. She recently mailed me a note along with a lopsided mug I had made at the retreat, which she had fired. In the note she said, "Anytime you do a sermon about the potter's wheel, I'll be happy to come and do it again."

You too can find a way out of the hamster wheel. It is different for each person, but there is always a way. When you fly on an airplane, the crew tells you to look around for the emergency exit signs and become aware of the closest way out. They tell you that if you are sitting next to an exit and don't want to be in charge of opening it in an emergency, you should switch your seat with another passenger. Sometimes we don't know how to get out of a situation. We may need to look around, perhaps in a different direction, for a way out that we didn't know existed. Sometimes we know the way out but are too scared to open the hatch. We need someone else to help us through the exit process. When we're looking for a way out, it's important to remember that God loves to provide us with trap doors, passageways to freedom, unexpected rides "outta here." God is a master at leading his people out of bondage.

Scripture tells us that "no testing has overtaken you that is not common to everyone. God is faithful, and he will not let you be tested beyond your strength, but with the testing he will also provide the way out so that you may be able to endure it" (1 Corinthians 10:13).

A way of escape! God got the Hebrews out of Egypt in the book of Exodus. He got Daniel out of the lion's den without a scratch. God rescued Noah, David and Esther and her people. He rescued the prostitute from being stoned, the paralytic from immobilization, the widow who wept for her only son from overwhelming grief. God makes a way of escape that we might be able to bear it.

Often for people in the hamster wheel, clear paths of circumstantial escape are the first step to health and well-being. We may need to move out of an abusive relationship. We may need to stop perpetuating an addictive cycle. We may need to be more honest with ourselves, others and God about what is actually going on. We may need a weekend of retreat and prayer. We may need intensive therapy so we can work through trauma, loss or pain. We may need spiritual direction to help us find our call.

We may need to change our priorities in the direction of love and service rather than frenetic activity and debilitating stress. We may need to seek out a friend or family member who will put us up for a while. We may need someone to show us where the exit signs are in our lives.

Trying to be a better person is not a way of escape. It most often is a choice motivated by an unhealthy desire to "fix" a hamster wheel situation, and it will go nowhere. It is like being chased by a monster in a dream. You can climb a tree, jump over the fence, even shoot the monster, but because it is a dream, he still keeps coming at you. Then you wake up! Being awake puts you in a completely different place, a danger-free zone with no monsters. Similarly, to leave the hamster wheel you must move into a completely different frame of reference, vertically out of the maze with no exit to a new place where you recognize God as liberator and intimate lover. This is the place where you can grow, learn and live freely without fear of attack.

One young woman I met with was a lawyer with two small children. She told me with tears that her husband, also very successful professionally, was a rage-aholic. He would corner her and yell in an outrage for long stretches of time, leaving her shaking and sick to her stomach. This had been going on for years, but recently it had escalated. Deeply committed to Christ, she kept praying for him and for guidance about what to do. In prayer one day, she invited Jesus to come into the scene in her mind where her husband had cornered her and was yelling. She saw Jesus quietly come alongside her and put his arm around her shoulders. Then he turned her away and together they walked out of the room together. A way of escape!

This woman's story got me thinking that we never escape the hamster wheel alone. We escape because God's arm is around us, leading us out of bondage and pain into safety, liberty and dependence on him. Just as the newly liberated Hebrew people had the pillar of fire and cloud with them in the desert, so in our desert of formation we can bear it because we are not alone.

Another example of a way of escape is illustrated by a couple with three children who had come to the United States from Australia. They had been separated for the better part of a year and divorce was imminent. The woman, who was living in Oregon, admitted to me that she had been critical and domineering as she tried to "lead her husband to the Lord." Separation, blow-ups and scattered fragmented relationships were chronic issues that she couldn't seem to resolve. One day in church, she had an experience of Jesus' love that told her she was supposed to move back to the area where her husband lived and just wait. After praying with others and talking with pastors and counselors, she jumped, in radical faith, completely out of the hamster wheel and moved herself and her children. In desperate faith she acted, even when it was very scary. Waiting was the worst of all. She knew she wasn't supposed to criticize her husband. She wasn't supposed to judge, manipulate or witness. She was just supposed to wait.

This was extremely difficult, especially when she discovered that her husband was living with another woman. She asked for prayer for strength and trust in God, even on days that seemed impossibly gloomy. Gradually, over time, as the couple shared childcare responsibilities and they saw more of each other, the husband realized that he still loved his wife. Together they committed to work on their issues, spend time together, communicate and grow. It wasn't easy for them to get on the potter's wheel and begin, but today they are reaping the fruit of their collaborative effort to get in step with their own transformation.

Once you have found your way of escape, several things will happen as you begin to grow and change. The next chapter will discuss several key actions we take that facilitate the change we seek. For those of us who are Christians, these action steps will sound familiar – we've read about these principles in the scriptures and talked about them in church. Concepts like: the need to confess wrongs, ask God to help us, and even make amends when we are wrong. The beauty of the twelve steps is that they have taken these principles and developed a tool to help us take these steps in a systematic, comprehensive manner.

I'm told that massage therapy "gets the kinks out" of our bodies, realigning and soothing tight muscles that actually cause us to get all crooked skeletally. I had a massage recently, and it was fantastic. Someone else with great expertise knew how to knead and pull and prod and poke me back into a healthy, pre-stress shape. It's tempting to think that hopping onto the potter's wheel is a lot like getting a massage. And, it kind of is. But there is also some cooperative work we participate in as the potter has his way with us. That's what we are going to talk about in the next chapter.

Chapter 11

Confessing and Requesting

by Teresa McBean

One of my favorite stories is found in the first book of the Bible—Genesis 18. Three strangers came to visit Abraham. It seems as if two were angels, and one was the Lord himself. The Lord prophesies his return in one year and promises that Abraham's wife, Sarah, will birth a son by the time he returns. Sarah is doing what any good wife would do. She's eavesdropping. She hears the Lord's pronouncement, and she laughs! Sarah has been barren her entire life. She and Abraham "were already old and advanced in years," according to this account. Evidently Sarah thought bearing a child at her age was utterly preposterous. She was worn out. Her husband was old. Certainly it was too late to hope for the satisfaction of bearing a child. (If you've read the story you know that she does get pregnant.)

But that's not my favorite part. My favorite part is when she failed to admit her laughter. The Lord asked Abraham why Sarah laughed. She lied and said, "I did not laugh."

The Lord said, "Yes, you did laugh."

"I did not!"

"Did too!"

"Did not!"

"Did too!"

I chuckle every time I picture this exchange. I think this is the first "He said/she said" conversation recorded in history. I review this story every time I am about to work Step 5. Like Sarah,

I have trouble "admitting" things to God, to myself, and to others. I'm not sure which is the toughest part—myself, God, or another human. I simply have trouble "admitting" things—even things that aren't all that bad.

Sarah laughed. That's all. Was that so bad? A critic might say it was an indication of her lack of faith in God. Maybe so. God had promised she would have a child. Why didn't she believe God's messenger? If you and your husband were way past the average childbearing years and someone told you that you were going to have a child, wouldn't you be tempted to laugh (or cry, depending on your view)? Did she know the stranger was actually the Lord? Perhaps she did. But hasn't God spoken promises to you that you haven't believed? Aren't there rich truths of hope and healing in God's word that you have ignored or that you believed applied only to others? I think we can extend Sarah some grace. I hope you will also be gentle with yourself during this process.

THE FIFTH STEP

This next step in the journey goes like this: We admit to God, self, and others the exact nature of our wrongs. This is tough work. If we ask, God will eagerly grant us the strength and willingness to do this step, but it's still a painful step. My prayer is that you will find the right person to listen to your inventory.

Most unhealthy family systems share a common goal: never let 'em see you sweat. That's another way of saying that "the best defense is a good offense." In families with hurts, habits, and hang-ups (that include all families, if we're honest), admission is sometimes viewed as a weakness. Why is admitting the error of our ways so tough? Unhealthy family systems are usually not safe places to reveal a weakness. Unhealthy families tend to be chaotic, capricious, and inconsistent. They can be rigid and rule-driven or without guidance entirely. Love in such families is conditional and life is unpredictable. Discipline is sporadic and sometimes cruel.

Even in healthy families, children can learn (usually due to unintentional teaching) that being yourself is not a good idea. When I was a child, I loved to read. I was so excited about the wonderful world of books! I couldn't wait to share what I learned from my reading every night during dinner. I assumed everyone would be as thrilled as I was by my adventures through the written word. As an adult, I look back on that time and realize how boring that must have been for everyone else. In my enthusiasm, I recounted every plot twist and detail of that day's book. I thought I was sharing a priceless gem. My family did not share this view. They teased me about my reading. They rolled their eyes and laughed. Soon I stopped sharing. No one intended any harm. They just wanted a moment of peace. But, from my child's view, I concluded that I was not safe in this family of teasers. I think it served as confirmation of a vulnerability all humans experience, a fear that we are "less than." I developed a strongly held conviction that something was broken within me and being myself was not a good thing.

So I ask you: was I a kid, teen, young adult, middle-aged mom, who was willing to admit a shortcoming? Certainly not! I learned, as many of us do, that to share the "real me" invites shaming—intentional or otherwise. If we learn that being ourselves is not okay, how much harder is it to admit when we have been our "bad" (or wrong, or mistaken, or simply less than the best) self? I cannot adequately convey the beauty of the cleansing experience I had when I shared with God, myself, and another for the first time. Admitting the exact nature of our wrongs is a hard thing to do. It is made tougher by past admissions gone wrong. But in the right environment—having come to know the awesome, loving God of scripture—it can be a comforting time of healing. Listen to how the biblical text talks about confession:

> Are you hurting? Pray. Do you feel great? Sing. Are you sick? Call the church leaders together to pray and anoint you with oil in the name of the Master. Believing-prayer will heal you, and Jesus will put you on your feet. And if you've sinned,

you'll be forgiven—healed inside and out. Make this your common practice: Confess your sins to each other and pray for each other so that you can live together whole and healed. The prayer of a person living right with God is something powerful to be reckoned with. (James 5:13-16 The Message)

CONFESSION, COMMUNITY AND CHOOSING WISELY

One day I confessed a pretty minor shortcoming in church. I told a silly story about how I was bad at remembering to attach a document when sending out an email. I told this in the context of a message I was teaching on grace. My point had to do with love covering a multitude of sins. I shared with the congregation how my entire team knew that I was a goof about this. I'd send out an email and tell them something was attached, and they'd send back a reply asking if it was written in invisible ink. My shortcoming, I reported, has to do with a lack of attention to detail. But my team loves me anyway. That was my point. But I think God had a different point. Since the day I confessed this shortcoming, I have remembered to attach documents I send out most of the time. Weird. Now sometimes I get emails back saying, "Hey, what's up with you? You attached your document!" Through this event, God reminded me that when we confess something and bring it into the light, powerful things happen. I desire to admit my shortcomings more than ever because I have been given a superficial but powerful-to-me example of the power of God to work through even the silliest of confessions. I don't know why or how this change in my ability to attach a document to an email occurred, but I know who made it possible. God is in the business of restoration. He is Rapha God—healing us, one stitch at a time (Rapha is Hebrew meaning healing, one stitch at a time).

Choosing someone to hear your confession needs to be done with care. Make sure it is someone with whom you can be frank, open, and honest. Ideally, it is best to share with someone who has worked through the 12-step process. If you don't know anyone with 12-step experience, look for someone who is willing to be available, who listens well, and who can relate to your struggles. I think it's important for the person to be the same gender. Sometimes this person may need to speak a word of encouragement and accountability, so it's best to find someone to whom you are willing to listen. The most important aspect of the admission process is to eliminate secrecy. It's a challenge to admit the exact nature of our wrongs. That's why it is important and very beneficial to have an experienced listener. As we go down our fourth-step inventory, our encourager will need to help us stay on track. New insights will be revealed and we will need to add them in writing to our original inventory. An excellent listener will be tuning in to hear the exact nature of our wrongs. After listening to our feelings of resentment, anxiety and fear, hearing our reactions and patterns of responding, and reading our lists, we will have a much-improved working knowledge of ourselves. Trust me, it will be a huge relief to have shared this with God, self, and another.

Mike O'Neill suggests in his book, *Power to Choose*, that we finish the fifth step and go off by ourselves and take time for quiet, prayerful reflection. He recommends reviewing the first five steps and then making time to be alone with God. As we read and review, we must listen for God's voice. We may need to add something to our list, go back to our trusted listener, and tell that person what we forgot. Once we can honestly say that the process is as complete as possible at this time, the fifth step is finished!

As an example of how telling the truth about the exact nature of our wrongs can make a difference, consider this statement from an interview with Corrie ten Boom. She spent many years in a Nazi concentration camp. She was a Christian, imprisoned for being a sympathizer to the Jewish people. This is what she says about telling the truth:

> The special temptation of concentration-camp life—the temptation to think only of oneself, took a thousand cunning forms. I knew this was self-centered, and even if it wasn't right, it wasn't so very wrong, was it? Not wrong like sadism

and murder and the other monstrous evils we saw every day. Was it coincidence that joy and power drained from my ministry? My prayers took on a mechanical ring. Bible study reading was dull and lifeless, so I struggled on with worship and teaching that had ceased to be real. Until one afternoon when the truth blazed like sunlight in the shadows. And so I told the group of women around me the truth about myself— my self-centeredness, my stinginess, my lack of love. That night real joy returned to my worship.[5]

Once we find a community where we can establish support systems, our work can continue. It's not enough to sincerely want God to mold and shape us. We need to show up for the work. The book of Philippians is a great comfort to me, especially this verse: "God is the one who enables you both to want and to actually live out his good purposes." (Philippians 2:13 CEB)

I love knowing that God is at work in me, giving me both the desire and capacity to live out his good purposes. Think about it. If we've turned our lives over to his care (step three), then our purpose for life is established: we live to carry out his good purposes. This is a big deal. Many of us don't feel capable. We have track records and a well-established history of living on planet earth that teaches us all sorts of things about NOT giving or receiving good. But, if we've taken the third step, we're on a journey of re-minding, re-membering...learning new ways to think, do, feel, and "see" the world, and our part in it.

One more verse to encourage us. "...be transformed by the renewing of your minds so that you can figure out what God's will is – what is good and pleasing and mature." (Romans 12:2, CEB) In the middle of suffering and self-doubt, I find this hard to believe. But my process requires that I remain curious and open to the possibility that when God says something, he means it and we can trust him.

---

5. Corrie ten Boom, *The Hiding Place*, (Bantam Books, 1971), pp. 27-28.

THE SIXTH STEP

But we have issues. In recovery, we call them defects of character or shortcomings. We cannot use one of our old coping strategies and deny, ignore, or blame others for this condition. It is our condition; we are not terminally unique; it is part of the human condition. Whatever we choose to call them, character defects are those undesirable parts of ourselves that must be removed if we are going to be our real, God-created selves. They are our faults, weaknesses, shortcomings, failings, limitations, manipulations, obsolete survival skills—the parts of us that make us cringe with embarrassment and shame. Conversely, we may be in denial about these not-so-hot parts of us. Eventually, transformative work requires willingness to acknowledge each of these limitations. Part of the process is consciously choosing to ask God to remove them; this is the work of staying on the potter's wheel long enough for the potter to accomplish his creative redesign work.

After the challenging work of confession, we move on to step six: (We were entirely ready to have God remove all these defects of character.) What do you think it means to be "entirely ready" to have God remove our defects of character? If we know our defects, and want them gone, what does it take to be "entirely ready?"

A timid knock on my office door introduced me to a young woman who knows what it means to be "entirely ready." It had been two years since she made her escape from a family system riddled with substance abuse, physical abuse, and neglect. In the beginning, it was hard. She missed her family, even though she knew something was wrong at home. She left to save herself, but sometimes she wondered why. Eventually she met the man of her dreams—or so she thought. Instantly she felt a cosmic connection and she just knew that he was the one for her. Such assurance and confidence in her newfound love emboldened her, and she joyfully accepted his suggestion to move in together at her place. It made such perfect sense. They'd save more money and would get around to getting married someday soon. No rush, really—after all, he was her destiny.

Until she got pregnant and he split. Sometimes he came around, and she was thrilled. She decided that the pregnancy was indeed a shock to him, and he just needed time to sort things out. The only certainties for her were these: he was her destiny, and he would return soon. Friends told her he had acquired a new love, but she decided they were just jealous of this special bond that she shared with the love of her life. She told them: "If you only knew how he treats me when we're alone, you'd know how much he loves me!"

She continued to be "entirely ready" to accept his lame excuses and erratic behavior. Months passed. She waited patiently for the return of her destiny. When the baby arrived, he showed up and got a big kick out of pointing out his newborn son to family and friends. She smiled with delight. She thought to herself, "I was right! I knew he'd return."

Unfortunately, he forgot to pick them up from the hospital and she felt totally humiliated. She called a friend to come take her home. She thought that there was no limit to her shame until she walked in the apartment and found her knight with another damsel. When the dust cleared and all the company fled, she confronted him. She'd never done this before and was shocked when he smacked her hard across the face, almost causing her to drop her newborn infant.

She now tells me that it was at that moment when she realized that she might have left the abusive home in which she grew up only to recreate it with this man. She wants to know what suggestions I have for her. She doesn't want to end up like her mother. She says that she is open to any ideas I might offer her except one: she cannot live without this man. She is "entirely ready" to do anything it takes to help him understand that she is the one for him. She would also like for him to stop reminding her so much of her own father.

She shook her head in confusion and said that she just doesn't get it. She doesn't know how to be "entirely ready." I assure her that being "entirely ready" is one of the things she does best. I pointed out her readiness to accept this man as her savior. In so doing, she willingly submitted herself to him. At this point in time, this young woman has spent one entire year being "entirely ready" to live any way this man dictated.

So here's a hard question: who or what are you "entirely ready" for? Notice that this step does not say "entirely ready" to go to any lengths to remove my defects of character. Some of us have been ready and willing to be done with our defects of character for a long time. That's not what this step says. It says: "entirely ready to have God…"

Are we "entirely ready" to let God be in charge of our lives?

Are we "entirely ready" to let God do for us what we have never been able to do for ourselves?

Are we "entirely ready" to have God transform our lives from the inside out?

It really would be a sight to behold if all of us were as ready to have God as this young lady was to have the man of her dreams. Apart from God, we can do nothing. We can be as sincere, as passionate, as purposeful as anyone has ever been. But on our own and independent of God, we are incapable of self-transformation. Only God transforms. Only God saves. Only God frees us from the bondage of trying to save ourselves. Only God can accomplish the complete rebuilding of self. What this step is asking of us is this: believe that without God's help, we can do nothing. Then, prepare to accept his help.

THE SEVENTH STEP

Once we've done the work of readiness, we are ready for the ask. (Step 7: We humbly asked him to remove our shortcomings.)

I didn't grow up believing in shortcomings. In the 1970s and 1980s, for example, we were reading books like *I'm Okay, You're Okay*. In my psychology classes I studied theories about human development, and most of them seemed to indicate that my parents had done something to mess me up (which is a little incongruent with being okay). B. F. Skinner, a noted behavioral psychologist of the day, reportedly raised his kid in a box! The underlying belief was that we are born blank slates, and if people write on us carefully, we grow up into productive, reasonably happy humans. I was in my twenties, so I liked all these theories. I liked the idea that if someone found a shortcoming in me, it was someone else's fault—bad writing on the blank slate.

Then I grew up and birthed babies. Those theories didn't sound so great once I became a parental unit. I didn't birth a blank slate, in spite of my best intentions. We met our firstborn for the first time in the delivery room. Her dad, fearing that the bright lights of the operating room would hurt her newborn eyes, shielded her eyes with his hand as she gazed upward. She crinkled her forehead and studied us with rapt attention. We hadn't had a chance to whip out our chalk and write on her slate, but we soon discovered that this look was vintage Meredith. (I might also add that her dad has been busy "shielding" her from harm—as best he can—ever since our initial meeting.)

Our second-born also came mysteriously prewired. That kid slept all the time. He loved to sleep. Initially I thought it was because we gave him a pacifier. He gave up that pacifier years ago, but that young man still loves to sleep! He's just a laid-back kind of guy.

My third pregnancy was a challenge. I worried during the day because the baby never moved. I couldn't sleep at night because he kicked and carried on. He's all grown up now, and he is still a nocturnal creature. For his birthday he asked for a bike, so he can get more exercise—by riding his bike at night through the streets of Nashville! (You can imagine how, as a mother, I was tempted to include bubble wrap with the gift.)

Three kids with the same parents, and each child is very, very different. I'll bet you have stories like mine as well. Not only did the "blank slate" theory not pan out, but it wasn't long before the "born good only to be ruined by your parental units" theory also took a hit. Our kids weren't always good, and sometimes I couldn't find a way to blame myself or my spouse for their bad behaviors. (I tried.) Maybe our family is different from yours, but we weren't okay all the time either. So we had three theories ditched: the "blank slate" theory, the "I'm okay, you're okay" theory, and the "it's always the parents' fault" theory.

Once we set aside all need to blame and judge ourselves and others, torture ourselves with unanswerable questions like, "Why me?" or "Whose fault is this?", we can turn our attention to thinking about the nature of a shortcoming. Shortcomings are anything in our lives resist change and seek control. They are those traits that restrict and block the work of the potter.

One of my friends in recovery told a story that made an interesting distinction between a defect of character and a shortcoming. (I know not all people make this kind of distinction in the recovery world, but it has helped me so I will share it.) He says that a defect of character is like a pro baseball player who runs slowly. No matter what he does, he cannot run any faster; he's tried. He is great at lots of things—hitting and catching and throwing and sliding—but kind of below par in speed. That's a defect. But his shortcoming is this: the guy keeps trying to steal bases, even though his coach asks him not to. That's a shortcoming. He's not willing to accept his speed limitations. Notice in this story that because of all his marvelous qualities, he's still on the team. But he makes a better team player if he plays the game conscious of his limitations.

Scripture has a bit to say about shortcomings too. It eliminates the need to rationalize, justify, or shift blame. In Genesis, the first book of the Bible, it says: "…every inclination of his heart is evil from childhood" (Genesis 9:21). God says this is the nature of man. This is the same God who looked at the work of creation—mankind—and decided it was "very good." This is a paradox. We were pronounced "very good" by God himself, but we have a predisposition to live independently of God.

Evil at its core can be defined as any time we live independently of God. We were created by God to live in an awesome, intimate relationship with God and with each other. But we have a predisposition to grow forgetful. We forget that there is a God and, more importantly, we forget that we are not God. As we forget God, we lose sight of how much we are loved. We grow insecure and look for love in all the wrong places. We also forget, or are never told, that we are born for a purpose, with a grand epic adventure set out before us by God. This leads us to look for meaning and significance in all the wrong places. Both of these by-products of forgetful living result in shortcomings. This is why we develop character defects. And here's the real kick in the pants: we, at birth, are vulnerable to wounding. So it's not okay to simply look around for someone to blame for our shortcomings. I have come to believe that it is less important for me to know how I developed these hurts, habits, and hang-ups than it is for me to simply acknowledge that they exist. As you've worked through these studies, that's exactly what has happened in steps 4, 5, and 6.

Step 7 is a really terrific one. We're asking God to do for us what we cannot do for ourselves: to remove our shortcomings. I love this verse: "For the eyes of the Lord range throughout the earth to strengthen those whose hearts are fully committed to him" (2 Chronicles 16:9, NIV). Think about it. Holy God is eagerly looking for us, but why? So that he can find the ones who aren't obeying him and punish them for their decidedly not-okay ways? No. So that he can find out who is behaving well and pat them on the head? No. God is looking for someone, anyone, who is committed to him—so that he can strengthen us.

God wants to strengthen us. God who is all-knowing, eternal, king of kings and lord of lords, ruler of the universe and the unseen world, all-powerful, all-everything God wants to strengthen us. He wants to do an extreme makeover, because each of us needs one. We are not okay. We are not blank slates. We are humans. We are prone to wander and forget that there is a God—much less desire to follow hard after him. All we have to do is ask. These are the practical practices that we put into place when we are consenting residents abiding on the potter's wheel.

Chapter 12

Inspired by Our New Way of Living, We Handle Our Wrongdoing Differently

by Teresa McBean

Broken relationships usually result in some form of banishment, and banishment is a terrible thing. Either we avoid others, or they avoid us. If we do have contact, it is usually stilted and awkward.

If you study the lives of David, Absalom, and the rest of David's extended family (2 Samuel 14 is part of that saga), I believe you will discover that banishment happens simultaneously in both the seen and unseen worlds. Broken relationships with God have an impact on our ability to love others. And broken relationships with others have an impact on our ability to draw near to God. It's hard to hop up onto that potter's wheel if we fear the hands of the potter. We weren't created to cope well with banishment. We were created to carry within our hearts a huge capacity to receive and to give love. One of our primary purposes is to dispense this love with boundless enthusiasm and generosity of spirit. Life experiences may influence our thinking on this subject and cause us to doubt the veracity of this principle, but it is true. Anxiety, frustration, resentment, guilt, and shame are all emotions that can result from banishment; they are certainly an unwelcome part of life.

In 2 Samuel 14, we are reminded that God doesn't take away life. God doesn't put us in a self-protective bubble. Sometimes we allow ourselves to believe that once we become a follower of God, life should get easier. That would be awesome, but we just can't support that theory based upon scripture.

Although life may not get easier, it can get better. One of the ways God plans for us to have a more abundant life is by teaching us how to live with the messiness of life on planet earth. When we find ourselves in the midst of a broken relationship—banished in some way—God teaches us how to restore relationship. Subsequent steps will provide more details about that process. This step deals with getting real about the banishment. All the steps are descriptors of how the potter works with his beloved clay.

THE EIGHTH STEP

In step 8 (We made a list of all persons we had harmed and became willing to make amends to them all.) we're going to make a list of all the people we've harmed, and we're going to become willing to make amends to each and every one of them. I'm sure it is tempting to digress on this point and distract ourselves with thoughts of how others have offended us. Don't digress. Hang in with the process. The old adage, "nothing changes if nothing changes," is a great principle to apply right this minute. Previously, most of us have preferred to ruminate over the wrongs others have committed against us. Scripture turns us around, though, and points us in a different direction. Listen to how Jesus talks about this:

> [Jesus says], "This is how I want you to conduct yourself in these matters. If you enter your place of worship and, about to make an offering, you suddenly remember a grudge a friend has against you, abandon your offering, leave immediately, go to this friend and make things right. Then and only then, come back and work things out with God. Or say you're out on the street and an old enemy accosts you. Don't lose a minute. Make the first move; make things right with him. After all, if you leave the first move to him, knowing his track record, you're likely to end up in court, maybe even jail." (Matthew 5:23-25, The Message)

If we're serious about trusting God, as we embrace the potter's wheel lifestyle, we become willing. Willingness starts with accepting full responsibility for our own lives and for the harm we have done to others. The previous steps help prepare us for this willingness. Most of us have patterns of blaming others, avoiding responsibility, and seeking retribution for the wrongs done to us. Willingness means we make it our job to focus on our own behaviors and to stop distracting ourselves with the shortcomings of others.

Trusting God's restorative work, we can tell the truth about how we have harmed others. This need not be a shame thing, as it might appear on the hamster's wheel. On the potter's wheel, because we are trusting God to forgive, restore and reshape us, harm is simply telling the truth. (That doesn't make it any easier, but I pray it will give us just enough courage to hold still on the wheel and live in the truth of our harming ways.) Harm is caused physically (e.g. injuring or damaging persons or property, financial irresponsibility resulting in loss for another, refusing to abide by agreements legally made, neglecting or abusing those in our care), morally (inappropriate behavior regarding moral or ethical issues, including: fairness, doing the "right thing," irresponsible behaviors at home/work/etc., ignoring the needs of others or usurping the welfare of others with our own selfish pursuits, infidelity, abuse, lying, broken trust), or spiritually (failure to live out our God-created identity to the detriment of others; failure to support and encourage that same kind of living in others.) The root of harm is usually selfishness. On the hamster wheel, we just recycle our pain. We either blame ourselves or others, we don't know what to do with our suffering, and so we keep suffering in the same way, the people we suffer with may change, but our experience does not.

On the potter's wheel, we learn about the concept of making amends, and we actually follow through and make them! Amends is the process of sincerely seeking to repair the damage we have done. In his book, *Power to Choose*, Mike O'Neill describes this as a two-step process: apology and restitution. Apology – "I was wrong." We tend to think of an apology as, "I am sorry." The problem with that sentence is its ambiguous nature. What are you sorry for? It can mean: "I'm a sorry no-good louse," "I'm sorry I got caught," "I'm sorry you're mad at me," or even "I'm sorry I have to deal with this." More drama doesn't make for a better apology. When we go to the shame-based "I'm sorry" place, sometimes we just fall all over ourselves and are willing to confess anything and everything for the sake of placating the person we have harmed. Making an apology isn't about confessing that which is not true.

Humans make mistakes, and some of them are whoppers. Admitting this is good. But that is not the same as shame-based amends, which merely says, "Hey, I am a sorry person." A heartfelt apology will include a deeply remorseful expression of regret for harm done. Accepting responsibility for the wrong behavior is the heart of an effective apology and can be a humbling experience. Think of it like this: it takes more character and integrity to go to a person and tell them the exact nature of the wrong done than to grovel with an expression of regret that is ill defined.

THE NINTH STEP

After we make amends, we are ready to make restitution. "What can I do to make this right?" Just saying we're sorry isn't enough, nor is it enough to decide for ourselves how to make things right. An apology without restitution is not amends. Sometimes restitution takes place before amends. If we owe back child support, pay it. If we can't make good on the full amount, then send what we can every month. Get real about what we can really afford. In situations where we fail to step up to the plate and live responsibly in the present moment, it is unlikely we will be given an opportunity to apologize. If we show some good-faith restitution, we may earn the right to be listened to. Remember to be willing to abandon all-or-nothing thinking. Perhaps we feel that the debt, financial or otherwise, is too large to repay. It is still important to ask the restitution question and proceed with restitution as best we can. (Amends and restitution are the heartbeat of step 9: We made direct amends to such people wherever possible, except when to do so would injure them or others.)

As a pastor, I am often privileged to hear people's stories. Many of them are tales of broken hearts. Most of them involve offensive behaviors and broken relationships. One consistent wish people express to me is a simple one: forgiveness. They want either to be able to extend forgiveness to those who have harmed them or they want to be able to receive forgiveness from those whom they have harmed. I have heard the same story from countless young men and women: Someone has violated their trust and no action has been taken to rectify the wrongdoing.

More than the act of violation of trust itself (which is serious enough), the fallout for individuals, families, and communities who do not have a process or skill set to deal with offensive behavior appropriately continues to heap insult on injury. In my experience, an offended person often desires to hear from his or her offender. They want the offender to acknowledge wrongdoing. But if an offender doesn't approach the amends process properly, more harm is done. Step 9 offers valuable guidance for amends making. (Speaking of guidance, make sure before taking these steps that you seek wise counsel from a spiritual advisor who understands the biblical principles and the twelve step model for recovery. This isn't the kind of thing you want to wing! As we are surrendering to the work of the Father, we are also seeking people to help us in our journey. This is a good step to seek guidance before proceeding.)

If we were created to live and love, then it seems to me that we are particularly damaged by any broken relationship. We long for reconciliation, even if we don't understand this need. We long to be given the opportunity to forgive. But forgiveness isn't a concept that we spend enough time teaching about in depth. We get forgiveness confused with forgetting; we think it means the same thing as full reconciliation. That's not quite correct. Forgiveness doesn't mean that we just forget the offense and resume life as if nothing happened. Forgiveness doesn't require us to put ourselves in dangerous situations with dangerous people. Forgiveness says that we are willing to transfer this case to a higher court—the holy court of God. In transferring it to God's court, we are asking God to do what he sees fit with the offense.

An effective step 9 is one step in the process of transferring the case to its proper jurisdiction. We ask for forgiveness, and we seek to make restitution. Sometimes we are forgiven and can make restitution; sometimes we are not forgiven, and our efforts to make restitution are rebuffed. Either way, when we offer to make amends, we are doing our part in the process of restoration.

I hope and pray that we will give people whom we have offended the opportunity to give us the gift of forgiveness. It is a burden to carry around that unopened package in our hearts. Hasn't our offense caused enough pain? Trust God. As we take responsibility for our part, we must allow God to take responsibility for the outcome. No matter what the results, we will be able to stand tall, knowing that we have been faithful to Him.

THE TENTH STEP

Steps 4 through 9 provided us with a way to clean up the messes of our past. But the truth is that messes will still happen. Step 10 (We continued to take personal inventory, and when we were wrong, promptly admitted it.) mercifully provides us with a way to deal with them as they occur. This is a huge blessing. Listen to what the *Big Book of Alcoholics Anonymous* says about step 10:

This thought brings us to step 10, which suggests we continue to take personal inventory and continue to set right any new mistakes as we go along. We vigorously commenced this way of living as we cleaned up the past. We have entered the world of the Spirit. Our next function is to grow in understanding and effectiveness. This is not an overnight matter. It should continue for our lifetime. Continue to watch for selfishness, dishonesty, resentment, and fear. When these crop up we ask God at once to remove them. We discuss them with someone immediately and make amends quickly if we have harmed anyone. Then we resolutely turn our thoughts to someone we can help. Love and tolerance of others is our code.[6]

Isn't this great? We now have an opportunity to practice these newly discovered skill sets, which is crucial if we want to live the abundant life that Christ has promised us.

When my children were small, they received inoculations against certain diseases. The shots were preventative medicine. Sure, they stung a little, but none of my kids have had polio, measles, mumps, rubella, or any of the other nasty diseases that felled so many children before the inoculations became available.

Step 10 is preventative medicine. It keeps us from falling back into the insanity, unmanageability, and dependencies that controlled us before we worked the twelve steps. Sure, it stings a little, but it can prevent the outbreak of a really bad disease. Recovery is a lifelong process—not something to turn on and off at our convenience.

These steps, when we apply them properly, are awesome. I'm reminded of 2 Timothy 3:16:

> "There's nothing like the written Word of God for showing you the way to salvation through faith in Christ Jesus. Every part of Scripture is God-breathed and useful one way or another—showing us truth, exposing our rebellion, correcting our mistakes, training us to live God's way. Through the Word we are put together and shaped up for the tasks God has for us."

I believe the 12 steps are particularly effective at helping us make

---

6. Anon., *The Big Book of Alcoholics Anonymous* (Alcoholics Anonymous World services, Inc., 2002), p. 84.

this passage of scripture a reality in our daily lives. As we are able to experience this transformation process, we change. But our natural inclination to forget God and our human proclivity to think "it's all about me" can cause us to get sloppy with our recovery tools.

My husband has one teeny, tiny flaw that I'm sure he won't mind if I share with you. He's not that great at putting tools away. I discovered this one spring day when our kids were young. He repaired one of their bikes and stuck the screwdriver he used in a nearby flowerpot. He promptly forgot that it was there. I think that screwdriver stayed in that planter for months. One day our youngest child overheard me asking Pete where our screwdriver was. Michael said, "Mommy, they're growing out back in their special pot." We can sometimes be like Pete, and get careless with our tools. If we aren't vigilant, we may return to our old habitual hamster-wheel lifestyle. This step helps us remember that we are in the hands of our heavenly Father, and from this position of safety, it's more than okay to admit wrongdoing; it is downright healing!

In our next chapter, Kim is going to talk about the process of transformation and how it's working in her own life.

Chapter 13

Allowing God to Mold Us

by Kim Engelmann

My son is growing bean plants for a science experiment, and they are lined up on his desk by the window. The plants grow toward the light. They are stretching, reaching, extending their little shoots toward that window to get as much photosynthetic power as possible. Unfortunately, human beings do the opposite. The world says, "Stretch away from God! You don't need him; after all, you are a self-made individual. Reach toward what is fun, self-gratifying and of the moment. This will make you happy" (it doesn't mention that these things are often futile, empty, and meaningless.)

Redirecting our lives can be painful, just like unclenching a fist hurts because the muscles have been constricted for so long. We aren't used to leaning toward God. We ache and stretch as we are pulled in a different direction. The result, however, of a posture inclined toward God is getting to know the self that was created for fellowship with him and to walk with God "in the cool of the day" (Genesis 3:8 NIV).

CHARACTERISTICS OF THE POTTER'S WHEEL

I have found in my experience as a pastor, as a teacher, and as a wife and mother that when God is at work to bring about transformation, suffering is somehow always involved. It is the nature of this fallen world that we must be broken, melted, and reshaped by the potter in order to be like Jesus. It is painful because we are naturally inclined in the wrong direction. But how do we know if we are suffering because the potter is working on us or because we're trapped in a hamster wheel? I have provided some guidelines in this section to help us discern the difference.

- God's work is not cyclical; it is revolutionary. Change

occurs. We get off the wheel in a different shape than when we got on.

• God's hand is involved in the process of formation. He is in charge and we are never alone, but it may get worse before it gets better.

• We may experience an awareness that we are being held and formed with loving intent. We may even get a glimpse of God's larger perspective regarding our call and purpose.

• The outcome brings new life for us and those around us. We have gone somewhere and become something new. Even if our circumstances remain unchanged, we have been liberated.

• We are not in a vacuum, nor are we in a "me and Jesus" endeavor. We have community: friends, pastors, counselors, therapists, lay ministers, recovery ministry community members and prayer warriors to help us through.

With the help of our support systems and the encouragement of the Holy Spirit, we grow and deepen even though we have a hard time doing it. Let's look at some of these ideas in more detail.

REVOLUTIONARY FORMATION

Think of a hamster running on his wheel. His focus is horizontal. He looks out through the wheel and sees his water bottle, the shavings, and the bars of his cage. As he cycles, he can focus only on his little world—its props and its comforts.

Now think of the potter's wheel. It goes around too, but if you are the clay, lying on your back, where are you looking? Up. And this makes all the difference. This vertical focus "turns our eyes upon Jesus" as we experience difficulty. This is not just a warm sentimentality or a nice thought for super spiritual people who have visions of Christ up in the corner of the ceiling. This is for ordinary people who offer themselves as living sacrifices on the altar of God's grace. In AA language, it is called surrendering to a "higher power" and acknowledging that we are powerless over alcohol. Knowing that we cannot do what we need to for ourselves, we focus on the One who can.

I have shared with you how the suffering l experienced after I came to California was qualitatively different from the suffering l had been cycling through before. My focus was on God and what he could do rather than on the situation itself. In my case, I had to change where l lived to get focused in the right direction. Through this, revolutionary change took place for Tim and me.

As we grow dependent on God, we find paradoxically that we have more agency through the gift of the Holy Spirit. We are not trying to be something we are not. We do not need to move the wheel. We do not have to deplete ourselves. Another is doing it for us, and he does a far better job. We are being fashioned for the purpose of holding the mystery of God's Spirit alive in us. He not only forms us but then fills us and enables us to be and do what we couldn't be or do on our own steam.

> "'Not by might, nor by power, but by my spirit, says the LORD of hosts" (Zechariah 4:6).

As God's hand touches us, we remain flexible under his gentle, intentional pressure. As we are formed we look into the eyes of the potter and know that we are loved beyond belief. As an infant looks into the face of her mother and begins to recognize her, begins to smile, so we focus on the face of eternal love. Through relationship with Jesus, we are changed, revolutionized, transformed into living in "the glorious liberty of the children of God" (Romans 8:21 KJV).

IT GETS WORSE BEFORE IT GETS BETTER

The reality that our situation can deteriorate before it starts to regenerate can keep many people from completing—or even starting—the healing process. We all want to avoid pain; it's a natural inclination. That's why there are so many painkillers on the pharmacy shelves. But the absence of symptoms is much different than genuine healing. Healing the pain of the past involves a pain of its own. It involves reliving excruciating experiences, and this can be extremely difficult.

I am a strong advocate for therapy. I constantly refer people to therapists whom I trust and who have a strong personal faith of their own. I also recommend that survivors of abuse receive long-term therapy. Quick fixes for complex cases and severe trauma are like taking an Advil for a brain tumor. Life has taken its toll. It has taken a long time to get where you are. You need at least half as long to heal, and healing can be painful.

Therapy covers some rough terrain, especially if you have experienced a lot of grief or trauma. It is necessary to go back and excavate, to work through the trauma layer by layer with a safe person. A good therapist will know how much you can stand and will regulate the process accordingly so it doesn't destroy you. This gentle, consistent excavation paves the way for healing. Gradually space opens up inside you, and your head begins to clear. Old habits and norms are reworked into new ways of relating and of being in the world. Gradually you are freed to love, live and enjoy. The challenge is to hang on when the journey involves a good deal of emotional turmoil. Revisiting old feelings and dark moments helps you realize that, one, you are not alone, and two, you have not been destroyed by the pain. You are bigger than the trauma, more resilient than the pain, and your journey is bringing you out, not pulling you under. Eventually, the cobwebs clear and you begin to see through the clean, clear lenses of recovery and healing.

At this point, new options emerge. New energy becomes available as you stop working, either consciously or unconsciously, on the old patterns and start exploring wider horizons. This takes time, it takes tenacity, it takes a deep resolve to grow and heal despite the hurdles that must be overcome. In all this we must remember who God is—a companion on the way, a liberator, a healer, a restorer of souls, a rebuilder of ancient ruins and the maker of meaning and purpose in our lives.

Stepping out of the hamster wheel involves breaking an addictive cycle, and it can come with withdrawal symptoms similar to those associated with drug and alcohol addiction. We may need to "withdraw" from being people pleasers who enable. Or we may need to extract ourselves from frenetic activity, staying busy for busyness's sake. In doing either we may encounter a sense of emptiness that we must confront before we can heal. This is not easy. It is painful but well worth the journey. For many, the hamster wheel is simply too familiar to leave-better the hell you know than the abyss you don't. New ways of interacting with the world and with others are too scary
to embrace. Lack of violence, predictability, healthy loving relationships, time for oneself, a purposeful and centered way of life may just be too threatening.

We have a pet bird, and her cage desperately needed to be cleaned one day. I didn't have time to do it at the moment so I let the bird out of the cage to experience the freedom of the back room. I thought it would be a relief for her to have more space and a cleaner environment for a little while. The phone rang just after I opened the door of the cage and, leaving the bird flying around the room, I went to answer it. When I returned, the bird was back in her dirty cage, sitting on her splintered swing. Freedom was unknown and scary. The dirt, the scuffed-up mirror and the poopy perch were all she had ever known. Like that bird, we often associate safety with what we already know, even if it is far less than what God wants to give us.

Jesus was always calling people to experience what they didn't know already.

"Come follow me and I will make you fishers of people."
"Be my witnesses."
"Go ahead, Peter. Come to me walking on the water. When you slip up, I'll be there to catch you."

The fact that Jesus is there makes dangerous undertakings safe, but it may take time and practice for us to learn this truth and practice the spiritual disciplines associated with radical belief in a God who saves.

GOD'S HAND IS IN THE THICK OF IT

The last thing I want to do is to create a formula that looks good on paper but has no lasting value in people's lives. So keep in mind that these distinctions provide a general way of thinking to be weighed with discernment and prayer as you move in the direction of emotional health.

Generally speaking, God's presence makes itself known as a "hopeful intruder" when circumstances have gone belly up. If we are on the right wheel, we will have an experience similar to that of Jesus as he looked toward the cross, "an angel from heaven appeared to him and gave him strength" (Luke 22:43). It may take a while for this to happen, and the distinctions between the two wheels are not always neat and clean.

Clearly, in the mess of my childhood, grace invaded my life. I was in the hamster wheel with no way of physical escape, but I was assured that I was not alone. This was a form of spiritual escape for me even though I could not change my circumstances. I also think my experience of Jesus' love helped me get out of the hamster wheel when I was old enough. In this way, then, the potter's hand was on me even when I was in the hamster wheel. As Christ says in John's Gospel,

What is born of the flesh is flesh, and what is born of the

Spirit is spirit. Do not be astonished that I said to you, "You must be born from above." The wind blows where it chooses, and you hear the sound of it, but you do not know where it comes from or where it goes. So it is with everyone who is born of the Spirit. (John 3:6-8)

I can't tell you that if you are in the hamster wheel, God will never reveal himself to you. Sometimes he has to in order to get you out! I can't say either that if you are on the potter's wheel, God is going to be so real in every moment that you'll feel loving and super spiritual at every turn. No, Jesus suffered and felt as though God had forsaken him. But it ended in resurrection. There are no formulas, just general ways of thinking. So bear this in mind when I say that usually when you are being fashioned by God on the potter's wheel, you will feel sustained.

When you experience deep pain on the potter's wheel, this is good-it means you are not avoiding or denying but listening to yourself and to what is real. Even when hope seems like a distant relative, you have an awareness that you and God together are stronger than the pain, that it will not overcome you. Gradually, you begin to find confidence in yourself. Slowly, but surely you notice yourself crawling out of the pit you've been in, perhaps with some mud on your face, but zealous to move forward and use what you have been through for good. The desire to use your wounds to heal others is a sure sign of potter's wheel formation. Paradoxically, the pain builds your confidence and sense of who you are in Christ-it doesn't snatch your dreams away. Rather dreams become possible to realize in an atmosphere of freedom and inner peace wrought from genuine healing.

THE PRESENCE OF COMMUNITY

Community is another key sign that you are on the right wheel. You will find that you are able to receive encouragement from people who care about you, who are all around you representing Christ. But this movement into community may be difficult. Survivors have been taught, usually from childhood, that they've got to do it on their own. It is a whole shift—a courageous move—to be able to say, "I can't do it on my own. I need help from God and I need help from the people of God." Reaching out to others arrests the hamster wheel and turns on the light so we can see our situation in a new way. But reaching out can be so difficult!

I am reminded of the story from homileticsonline.com of David, an eleven-year-old boy in the Midwest who was run over by a tractor. He was significantly injured and blinded, and he could move only his right arm. For months he lay immobile in the hospital. Doctors said that he should have been getting better, but his refusal to respond to their efforts hinted at disillusionment in his spirit. He didn't want to try His mother sat and kept vigil with him. In the bed next to her son was a year-old baby boy who would not stop whining. He was agitated and upset, and nothing seemed to calm him down. One day, in desperation, David's mother picked up the fussy baby and placed the child right on her son's chest. At first David didn't respond. The baby fussed and moved uncomfortably. Then, slowly, David began to move his good arm. He lifted it for the first time since the accident and gently began to stroke the little boy's back. It was the beginning of his recovery, and a relationship developed between David and the infant that nurtured and healed them both.

Sometimes we've been so lambasted, crushed and bruised by life that we just don't care anymore. We can't try. We feel as though we can't change anything for the better, and we don't care that we can't. We become immobilized by the overwhelming flood of difficulty that we have experienced. So any effort to reach out, even a feeble one, can require tremendous energy. It can even signify desperation.

If someone reaches out to me, I assume as a rule that this may be their one and only attempt to get the help they need. The person may be drowning, and this may be their last chance to show me that they're going down. I swoop in with life rafts of supportive networks and helpful people. I sometimes overdo it, I know, and people kindly tell me that they just wanted to know when the grief and loss support group met, or how they could get a lay minister to visit a few times. I overreact because I know how difficult it can be for survivors to reach out. This may be the last time they act on the dim and fading hope that things can be different.

If someone comes to you for help, don't ever underestimate how hard it may have been for them, and respond with all the love you can muster. If you are the one who doesn't want to try anymore, my prayer is that you will reach out one more time or make an attempt for the first time. It can mean the difference between life and death. It can move you from hamster wheel to potter's wheel. Once you let others into your pain, they testify to the fact that not only is the potter forming you, he is also forming them and forming the church.

It is within this community of Jesus Christ that healing occurs. The church was called together at Pentecost as a human representation of the body of Christ. Therefore each of us must become acquainted with our own brokenness and walk alongside others who are also broken. This is what Jesus did. As we walk through suffering with one another, we remember that our true home is not here but in heaven where we will have perfect fellowship with God.

The mission and purpose of the Christian community is to be Christ to one another, walking in the way of the cross, bearing one another's burdens, invoking God's presence for healing and wholeness, yet always pointing to the ultimate victory that is ours as we move homeward to resurrection and perfect fellowship with our Creator.

VERTICAL FOCUS

Another sign that you are on the right wheel is that your gaze is vertical rather than horizontal. The circumstances surrounding you are important but do not determine your state of mind. Joy may come to you for no apparent reason. Your awareness of God shifts your priorities toward service, love, people and enjoying the moment. There is a willingness to surrender on the potter's wheel that is not apparent in the hamster wheel. There is a peace that is not passive but courageous-it is the courage to change the things we can and the discernment to know what we can't.

To change what we can, we might need to take drastic measures to make ourselves safe and begin again with new people in new ways. We might need to try out -of-the-box possibilities that we didn't have the courage to try before, or that we didn't even see. We might need to decide that what we thought was so important for so long, what we had been giving our lives to, isn't actually important after all. Pushing the "reset" button on priorities, living out of the divine center of grace and love, and knowing our purpose and call are all fruits of the potter's wheel. Suffering on the potter's wheel produces character (Romans 5:3-4).

NEW LIFE WITHOUT CIRCUMSTANTIAL ESCAPE

For many of us, there may be no possibility of escaping from our circumstances. Perhaps we are the caregiver for an alcoholic family member who is chronically ill as a result of his addiction. Perhaps we are a single parent struggling to make ends meet as, we wait for checks from a former spouse who refuses to work. Difficulty presents itself in countless ways, and life marches on. Sometimes it's all we can do to live one day at a time. I speak from my own experience. There was no way out for me growing up. One day when I was about 12 years old, I had been told too many times that I was evil, that I was not good enough for anyone to speak to and that my attitude was sending me to hell. In desperation I downed a fistful of aspirin and lay on the couch waiting to die. I couldn't even do that right. Nothing happened, and when I tearfully told my parents what I had done, they were outraged. I was ungrateful and rebellious - far more a loser than I had been before. I couldn't win. No one suggested that I needed counseling, or group therapy, or even a consistent youth group to attend. No one wanted to admit that there was a problem that was not me. The way out was barred, locked, shut. It appeared hopeless, until Jesus came in with his love. That was my escape from finite despair into infinite grace. I still suffered. I still went into depression in the hamster wheel. But I had something to hold on to after that experience: Jesus' presence in the midst of it. This kept me sane and alive.

In these instances, the way of escape may not be circumstantial. It may be spiritual. Peter was released from prison by the angel. He was free to go wherever he wished! Paul was imprisoned and actually awaiting execution as he wrote to the Philippians. Yet the way he wrote, you would hardly know it. He was full of the Holy Spirit, not oppressed or ground down by his circumstances. Philippians is the most joyful letter in the New Testament. Escape routes are sometimes circumstantial, sometimes spiritual, but they always move us toward freedom and purpose.

I knew a woman who had a son, Kyle, who suffered with severe cerebral palsy. Her suffering was not brought about by any sinful behavior, but it was still very difficult for her to cope. She could have found herself on a hamster wheel of over-responsibility and anger as she cared for her son. Yet in the midst of the pain, as she and others prayed, she and her family began to change. Gradually Kyle became a gift rather than a problem. The love he showed them, the way they learned about dependence on God through Kyle's dependence on them, the way they drew people into their lives and gave to so many - these were all testimonies of the potter's involvement in this family's pain. Redemption, healing and love told me that God was working. The focus was always more on God than on circumstances, their outlook was hopeful, and each moment with Kyle was precious.

I do not think God ordained Kyle to be sick. I believe that, ultimately, God wants everyone to be well, whole and complete. I do think, however, that the channels of God's grace overcame suffering to create greater love, joy, and right priorities in that family than if Kyle had not been born. Here there was no circumstantial means of escape. The family could have taken the advice of doctors and institutionalized their son, and yet for them (not for everyone), the right choice was to care for him. As they did they grew closer, fell more in love and relished the opportunity to share the faithfulness of Jesus with other families who had disabled kids. This is potter's-wheel formation. Here are some questions you can ask yourself when you are in a situation that provides no circumstantial escape:

• Where can I go to get ongoing, consistent prayer?

• How can I get support from others who are going through a similar experience?

• Where can I find a safe place to be authentic and share, without "lingo," what is really going on inside of me?

• What possibilities exist for ministry—for serving others out of my difficult experience? (Sometimes we need time, space and healing before we can even think about this. The last thing we want to do is serve others out of our own need to be served. But sometimes taking action like this promotes the healing process.)

• How can I discover new venues of expression and opportunity that will bring me joy and fulfillment? What will keep me from losing myself in this experience?

Do you see how these questions can move you out of the hamster wheel? Looking for the answers will shift you from isolation into community, from perilous places into safe places where you can be authentic. These questions encourage you to seek joy and opportunity and to move forward in relationship with God and others. These questions foster a sense of identity that is resilient, creative, and liberating.

I must say a word about safe places. Unfortunately, churches don't always qualify. One couple I know shared with their pastor that their son, who had been a missionary, had suffered a mental breakdown. The pastor responded that this had happened because of sin in their son's life, then he shooed them out of his office and never called them again. You can imagine that this couple became estranged from that church. For this pastor, a simplistic answer to a complex problem was all he could offer. He was threatened by the misery of the situation and decided that rather than deal with the pain of it, he would dismiss it from his mind.

It took this couple a while to find a safe church that addressed mental illness both from a sound spiritual perspective and a sound psychological one. Out of their hurt, confusion and longing for fellowship, they founded our church's HELP group for healing, encouragement, love and prayer. Be careful, discerning and prayerful before sharing with anyone. A good rule to remember is that Jesus is a lifter of burdens. He never lays on a bent back another weight. "A bruised reed he will not break." (Isaiah 42:3; Matthew 12:20).

NEVER IN ISOLATION

The importance of community, of being "all together in one place" (Acts 2:1), goes back to the disciples' emphasis on gathering together when the early church was formed. The very fact that God created the church reveals that he didn't mean for us to go it alone. We were meant to "bear one another's burdens, and in this way you will fulfill the law of Christ" (Galatians 6:2).

That's a pretty incredible law, if you ask me—holding one another up, keeping each other in prayer, doing "small things for one another with great love," as Mother Teresa said.

The movie *Awakenings* with Robert De Niro depicts people in a psychiatric ward who are completely immobilized. No one believes that these patients have any mental ability until a doctor played by Robin Williams begins administering a drug that wakes them up. Suddenly they can move, they can talk, they can interact with their families. Their old personalities return. Heartbreakingly, the drug's effects wear off, and the people eventually return to their inert state. This story is based on the true account of Oliver Sacks, who wrote about it in a book called *The Man Who Mistook His Wife for a Hat*. While the movie portrayed all of the patients returning to immobility, Sacks reports that in fact most of the people with one significant person in their life stayed awake and did not regress. This speaks strongly for the power of relationship, love and human contact. Our identity, our meaning and our desire to live comes out of meaningful relationships.

The church I am involved in tries to provide concrete ways for people to reach out and find help. We provide many recovery and support groups—quite a smörgåsbord, in fact. This is because we believe transformation happens in small groups that provide healing, prayer and a safe haven. We believe that God works through this network of support systems, all of which are staffed by laypeople who simply feel called to give back in the name of Jesus.

It has been shown that many people come to church for the first time simply because another person invites them. Sometimes all we need is one person who cares. Maybe you can be that person for someone else. Or maybe you can reach out to the one person who will be the difference between life and death for you.

Next up, we'll talk about the work of transformation.

Chapter 14

The Work of Transformation

Teresa McBean

Kim described in the last chapter various ways in which she experiences the potter's wheel lifestyle lived out in community. In fact, she says that living within community is a clue that we're on the right wheel. Proponents of the 12-step model believe the same. Pick up a "Big Book" and you'll find story after story featuring tales of drunks helping other drunks. (In case you haven't read it, let me say that this terminology is in no way meant to be demeaning. It is a way the community of "anonymous" speaks– as a humble reminder of where they've been, and where they can return if they grow complacent. It is also meant without an ounce of judgment. Because in AA, judgment isn't what they're about!)

THE ELEVENTH STEP

It's a paradox, really, this work of transformation. Because without time for solitude, I can attest to the fact that if I show up for community, even my tolerant, non-judgmental community might send me home for a grown-up timeout. The work of transformation is both solitary and communal. Without one, the other is ineffective. I cannot work out my salvation in isolation. But I cannot rely solely on my community to keep my head screwed on straight either. Within the context of the wisdom of potter's wheel living and the 12 steps is where prayer becomes a vital part of our restoration. It's at this point in the process that we enter our eleventh step: We sought through prayer and meditation to improve our conscious contact with God, praying only for the knowledge of his will for us and the power to carry it out.

"This book of the law shall not depart from your mouth, but you shall meditate on it day and night, so that you may be careful to do according to all that is in it; for then you will

make your way prosperous, and then you will have success."
(Joshua 1:8 NASB)

I wish I could honestly tell you that I embrace this perspective joyfully, but that would be deceitful. Some days, the woes of the world perch heavily on my shoulders, pushing me down into a lethargic pit of quiet and desperate apathy. On those days I am more drawn to solitaire than to prayer and meditation. I'm more likely to lay on the sofa and aimlessly click through the television channels using the least amount of energy required by the TV remote. I find all sorts of reasons not to pray. Since I'm a pastor, this tendency to zone out rather than focus on my conscious contact with God is embarrassing. But working a recovery program has taught me that vigorous honesty is essential. So there it is—I struggle to pray, even as I know that prayer and meditation is a key element of any spiritual program on the potter's wheel.

In recovery, I've also learned that the next right step doesn't require enthusiasm. Commitment to the journey is a daily expression of a lifelong process. It is a lifestyle. The eleventh step provides me with structure when my sincerity isn't enough to get me moving in a healthy direction. I am comforted when I realize that I am not alone in my resistance to receiving comfort from conscious contact with God. The psalmist certainly understood this when he wrote the following psalm:

> I lie in the dust, completely discouraged; revive me by your word. I told you my plans, and you answered. Now teach me your principles. Help me understand the meaning of your commandments, and I will meditate on your wonderful miracles. I weep with grief; encourage me by your word. Keep me from lying to myself; give me the privilege of knowing your law. I have chosen to be faithful; I have determined to live by your laws. I cling to your decrees. Lord, don't let me be put to shame! If you will help me, I will run to follow your commands. (Psalm 119:25-32 NLT)

No matter what season we find ourselves in, God is always in the mood to draw near to us. We don't have to be perky, perfect, and performance-driven in our pursuit of God. Even when we are broken, battered, and beaten down, God is available to us. Healthy relationships are like two-way streets. Two-way streets work because everybody follows the rules: driving on the correct side of the road, not crossing the yellow line, etc. Scripture is clear. God desires and seeks relationship with his children. Healthy relationships stay healthy when we follow the guidelines. God created us, and he knows how to relate to us. All good relationships are mutually satisfying. There is healthy give and take within those relationships. Prayer is a way we build a healthy relationship with God.

I haven't always understood what prayer means. In moving off the hamster wheel onto the potter's wheel, I have learned that prayer includes two essential elements. First, it includes an admission of our powerlessness (step 1). Why bother with prayer if we are our own god? Second, it includes an acknowledgment of our daily choice to accept God as our higher power and surrender to his restorative work (steps 2 and 3).

I've also discovered that another element of prayer involves meditation, which is a fancy way of saying that we are listening to God. Some believers are scared off by the term meditation, but do not fear! Meditation is a biblical concept.

> My meditation of Him shall be sweet; I will be glad in the
> Lord. (Psalm 104:34)

I love Mike O'Neill's personal description of contemplative prayer:

> "Let your body relax, and let all the tension and all the
> thoughts go out, and all the preoccupations. Either meditate
> on a small scripture or meditate on just one or two words. I
> meditate on Jesus, the Holy Spirit, or Abba Father (Romans
> 8:15). My mind will wander now and then, but I just return to

my beginning meditation and try to love God."[7]

Many voices compete for our attention: our culture, our family of origin, our false beliefs, and even the thoughts that spring up as a result of our tendency to live self-centered and self-seeking lives. Improving our conscious contact with God confronts the voices that seek to distract us from our God-created identity and purpose. We must replace the voices that historically have led us to unintentional, counterproductive behaviors. Nothing changes if nothing changes.

The conscious contact we seek here is far greater than a mere acknowledgment that God exists. It is about relationship. Relationships take work. I've been married for over 35 years. I know a lot about my husband, but every day, we make an effort to maintain conscious contact. My husband travels several days a week. At the end of every day and sometimes several times during the day, we talk. We take turns. One talks, the other listens. Some nights, one of us is more chatty than the other. But in the end, I think it evens out (he might disagree) because both of us are highly committed to a satisfying love relationship. If we didn't do this, we would lose our intimate connection. Relating to God is no different. We talk. We pray. And God listens. God talks and we listen—that's meditation.

Prayer and meditation is NOT about feeding the ego of a narcissistic, hungry-for-attention god. It's focused, especially when we recover from our spiritual sleepiness and awaken to the reality of our purpose for living. This is incredibly hopeful. After years of feeling "less than," hopeless, helpless, and downright naughty on the hamster wheel, it's taken some adjustment to realize that I am a person of value and that God believes in me. This is a big deal. Think about it. No longer limited to desperate cries for mercy, on the potter's wheel, while God is molding and shaping us, we can ask, "What are you up to, Papa?"

---

7. Mike O'Neill, *Power to Choose* (Sonlight Publishing, 1992) p 170.

My husband grew up in a home of believers. I did not. I always thought that in our marriage he would be the one who had the knowledge of God's will, and I'd have to rely on him to get it straight and explain it to me. I didn't believe that I'd be able to learn enough to acquire a working knowledge of God's will, much less acquire the power to carry it out. I was wrong. Read Romans 12:1-2. This scripture applies to all of us. We can come to know and do God's good, pleasing, and perfect will. God desires this for us. Often God wants this more for us than we desire it for ourselves. Don't let our old false beliefs shaped by shame and self-loathing keep us from celebrating this point: God wants us to know his will, and he desires to empower us to carry it out (Philippians 2:13). Isn't that incredible? Sometimes we wonder what we should pray. When in doubt, the eleventh step prayer for the knowledge of God's will and the power to carry it out is a surefire guarantee. It is completely within the will of God and within his power to answer it. God is not fickle. He will hear and answer our prayer. But I must admit that I have spent many an hour asking for God's will, meaning that I desire to know what God wants me to do. Recently I've come to appreciate that God tells me that my work is to believe in him (John 6:29). Knowledge of God's will is not just about what I do, but perhaps more about whom I "be." This has led me to conclude that God's will is always for me to know him. I've found that when I am aware of God's heart, my heart seems quite capable of figuring out what he wants me to do.

I don't know where you are today in your spiritual journey. Perhaps this is a good day and all is right with your world. I hope so. But if it is not, and if you are completely discouraged, weeping with grief, lying to yourself, faithless, and far, far away from God, know this: it is still a good day to practice the eleventh step. In the next chapter, Kim will continue our conversation on prayer.

Chapter 15

Discovering Potter's-Wheel Formation Through Prayer

Kim Engelmann

Jeffrey, a junior-higher involved in our church youth program, is an expert swimmer. He has broken records of all kinds, and he amazes those who watch him. People stand in awe and shake their heads as he swims-not just because of his speed and competency, but because this young man has a debilitating, progressive lung disease that may eventually prove fatal. In a sport that requires rhythm in breathing and good lung capacity, his excellence in swimming baffles. Many people are praying for Jeffrey's complete and total healing, and his parents are in a small group that provides support for the family. Discouragement, however, can set in.

One day Jeffrey turned to his Mom and asked, "Mom, why doesn't God just do a miracle?"

Without missing a beat, his mother turned to him and replied, "Honey, you are the miracle."

Suffering. It may not be alleviated. There may be no way to escape the pain of our circumstances. But through intentional prayer, miracles happen in the midst of our pain that remind us of the potter's presence and power.

I am aware that in writing about suffering, I am walking a tightrope. I want to adequately address all the foibles and pitfalls of our human condition that keep us in bondage to things that are not God's will. However, I do not want to over psychologize and under spiritualize. There is no doubt that God is able to do "abundantly far more than all we can ask or imagine" (Ephesians

3:20). No matter where we are, no matter how badly we have messed up, no matter what our story, our pain, our grief—there is a Redeemer. There is always hope because there is always Jesus. And hope comes about in different ways for different people. None of us know the outcome of our own story. Miracles happen, even when they are different from what we expected.

The power of prayer is real. I oversee a healing service at our church, a simple service with only 30 or so people who attend. We have Communion and then we pray individually for those who request it. There is no hype, no calling people to the front to "testify," no long-winded expositions; it is simply a brief meditation, Communion and prayer. This important gathering is one of the few times in a large church when people can spontaneously receive one-on-one care. I feel privileged that people allow me into their story, into their pain, and grant me the honor of praying for them. I can't believe I get paid to do it. In this service people are regularly healed. Many wonderful things happen very quietly. One person who needed jaw surgery received prayer and her jaw was realigned. She didn't need the upcoming operation. A woman who loved to hike had to stop because of back pain. As she was prayed for, her back stopped hurting. Now she hikes all over the place. Someone else asked for prayer for a son who had been hospitalized for several days with a serious internal rash. We prayed, and the next day the rash was gone. I took a member of our healing team with me to pray for a woman who was in a coma. As we laid hands on her the Holy Spirit's presence was palpable. In two days she was back home. I could go on.

People are also healed of their emotional pain. One person had grown up with severe abuse. It was ritualistic, and it took every form I had ever heard of. I was horrified as I listened to this individual share the awful abuse that had been present during childhood - every day, year after year. This person regularly attended the healing service, which was quieter, with fewer people, than the larger service and provided a greater feeling of safety. Communion was meaningful-one-on-one prayer essential.

Over the years that this person has been coming, healing has happened. Growth has occurred. It is not just the healing service that has helped. It is counseling, it is the men's fellowship, it is friends, it is this person's hard work to stay on track and be faithful in asking for help. This person now has a joyful demeanor, a centeredness that has replaced nervous agitation, and a light in the eyes. I am amazed that this individual has had the courage to keep coming, keep pursuing health and wholeness, keep moving forward.

If ever I forget, this service reminds me of the power of prayer and of Jesus' longing to make us whole and complete. In a lot of this stuff, we don't wrestle against flesh and blood. We have an Enemy and we can't get through life victoriously unless we know how to pray deeply and regularly. There is no substitute for prayer. If Jesus needed it, we certainly do as well. We may not understand everything we are up against in the spiritual realms, but we do know that Jesus is big enough and alive enough to take it all on for us. Getting to know him ought to be the extreme focus of our prayer life.

Although God can do anything, he asks for our cooperation and participation. He wants our input, our love, our investment. No prayer goes unheard by God, but the way we pray can shut him out rather than invite him in. There is a divine courtesy about Jesus. He is not pushy. An invitation must be given. There must be a place set aside so he can come in and sit down. The latch must be opened, the door swung wide. There must be a willingness on our part to encounter the Someone we have been "talking at" all our lives but may never have experienced with any intensity. This can be scary.

When I have company over that I don't know very well, I always feel a little awkward, harboring a slight fear that I will be disapproved of. Will my guests notice the stains on the carpet? Will they dislike my cooking? Will the conversation be easy, or will it be stilted and forced? Still, I go through with it, and each time I have those same people over, it gets easier and easier. I don't have to start from scratch. I already know them. I am developing a relationship.

I have found out that making space for Jesus is nothing less than making space for the best company you will ever have. There is no judgment, no disapproval, no raised eyebrow at the stains of my life. Rather, there is great appreciation for my invitation, and the conversation is always full of grace. There is centeredness and the feeling that Julian of Norwich expressed when she wrote, "All shall be well, and all shall be well, and all manner of things shall be well." Feeling this way unknots my need to control. I can surrender and thereby have time to really love-to love Jesus, to love my family, to love myself, to love others.

In order to make space for transformation in our lives, we may need to change the way we pray. I sure did. I realized at one point that I was doing a whole lot of talking and not much listening. I had always been "in charge," thinking I had to hold everything together through prayer. Realizing that I was not the one who made things happen in my prayer life was a huge hurdle that I had to overcome. And surrender does not come easily to me. As I have said again and again, changing old patterns is difficult. Trying something new feels awkward at first. Gradually, however, familiarity grows and the new way becomes less difficult, and then enjoyable.

When God asks Jeremiah to go down to the potter's house, Jeremiah observes that the pot being created is flawed. The result? The potter "reworked it into another vessel, as seemed good to him" Jeremiah 18:4). The clay at this point is still malleable enough to be reshaped. In the next chapter, however, Jeremiah buys a pot that has already hardened (Jeremiah 19). It cannot be reformed. Jeremiah throws the pot down and it breaks into pieces, illustrating the impending destruction of Judah and Jerusalem. The hardened vessel cannot be used for God's purpose, so it is destroyed.

Prayer is what keeps us moist in God's hands—pliable, flexible, moldable, usable. The rigid old patterns that would destroy us soften as we open ourselves to the presence of Jesus and make space for him in our lives, allowing him to take over. Here are some suggestions for prayer that can open us up to potter's wheel transformation.

MOVING FROM SOLILOQUY TO SILENCE

Rarely in prayer or Bible study groups does silence take precedence over words. It is easy for us to wax eloquent and demonstrate great spiritual verbosity, never stopping to hear what God might be saying back to us. Being silent before God is a hard discipline to pull off. People tell me that they can't do it. It's too hard. Their mind wanders, they think about taking the dog to the vet or how much mayonnaise to put in the chicken salad. "I'm not wired for this," they say. "It's just not me."

While silence is certainly easier for some than for others, it is a discipline that can be learned by anyone. Eugene Peterson calls it a "disciplined, intentional passivity."

Spending time alone with God is not meant to draw us back into isolation. While there may be times when we are called to "go to a deserted place" like Jesus did, the result is for us to be strengthened so we can go back into the world loving the way Jesus did - sacrificially and meaningfully. Henri Nouwen in *Making All Things New* puts it this way:

> Without solitude it is virtually impossible to live a spiritual life. Solitude begins with a time and a place for God and him alone. If we really believe not only that God exists but also that he is actively present in our lives - healing, teaching and guiding – we need to set aside a time and a space to give him our undivided attention.

Our silence in God's presence is a space that we give him so that our agenda can be replaced by his agenda. Hamster wheel prayers are noisy and may sound something like this: "Lord, I just thank you that I can come before you today and bring this list of requests to you. Please help so and so, and so and so, and also help me get everything done today to get ready for my housewarming party. I pray that you would get my son off of his duff and make him find a job. Be with everyone and bless them. Amen."

If we pray this kind of prayer, God certainly listens. He always listens. But sometimes we don't let God get a word in edgewise. It's all about us and what we think is important that day. Or we cycle through rote prayers, barely giving our words a thought since we have said them so often. I recently learned that until a few hundred years before Christ, it was against Jewish law to write out a prayer - any prayer that did not emanate from the heart was considered blasphemous. The apostle Paul tells us clearly that "we don't know how to pray as we ought" (Romans 8:26). Prayers that are effective and liberating are those that allow the Holy Spirit to pray through us. God's words become our words. His thoughts our thoughts. This happens slowly as we grow into learning how to listen and then receive God's agenda.

If the person praying the prayer above would take time to listen, she might begin to feel more love for her son, and perhaps a thought would come to her about how to interact with him in a helpful way rather than an angry way. Listening might help her to slow down and realize she has already done all that's necessary for the party. Jesus told Martha, "There is need of only one thing," to sit at his feet (a place usually reserved for the rabbi) and listen (Luke 10:38-42).

When we stop and listen, we often experience a shift in perspective. What seemed so important moments ago fades into the background. Other things such as Jesus' love and the people in our lives come into the foreground.

Here's another hamster-wheel prayer: "Lord, please make me a better person. I'm supposed to do what my husband wants, but I'm sick and he doesn't believe me. I had a fever and he made me prepare dinner. When I went to lie down he pulled the covers out from under me and I fell on the floor. I must be doing something awful to make him so angry. Help me be a better person. Amen."

This is the prayer of someone who is running in the wheel of abuse. It is the wrong prayer, even though it is a cry for help. Answered prayer in this case—becoming a better person—will provide no relief for the victim. Something will always be "wrong" with her. The abuse will continue and will escalate until she has the courage to leave. A prayer that might open her to change could be, "Lord, give me your thoughts and your Holy Spirit. Help me to see your perspective and your will in this situation. Lord have mercy on me. I open myself up to your care for me."

It is not that God doesn't hear the first prayer or won't help this person. If God didn't respond to flawed and misguided prayers, we'd all be in trouble. But an open-ended prayer in which we invite God's initiative is the way we find true refreshment. We don't find relief in controlling every minute we spend in God's presence. Rather than asking God to come up with the answers to our dilemma and telling him what the solution should be, it is better to ask him what he has for us and invite him to act accordingly.

I used to always pray at the end of my counseling sessions in a rote way that indicated we were done and it was time to go. It was a kind of escort out the door. I am getting to the point now where instead of plunging in with words that fill the air, I ask if it would be okay to spend a few moments in silence listening, inviting Jesus to come be with us. Then if words come, they come. If not, they don't. True prayer is inviting Jesus in, letting his words become our words, his thoughts our thoughts. By creating space in this way, the Spirit has the freedom to come intercede for us with "groans that words cannot express" (Romans 8:26). There is a depth of prayer that words cannot plumb. Remember the verses from Isaiah?

> Why do you spend your money
> for that which is not bread,
> and your labor for that which does not satisfy?
> Listen carefully to me, and eat what is good,
> and delight yourselves in rich food.
> Incline your ear, and come to me;
> listen, so that you may live. (Isaiah 55:2-3)

What gets us out of futility and circular effort? Listening for God's voice. Giving ear to what God has to say to us about our life and our call. Hearing God's song of love in our heart makes our soul live. As Julian of Norwich states,

> We are so preciously loved by God
> that we cannot even comprehend it.
> No created being can ever know
> how much and how sweetly and tenderly
> God loves them ....
> Therefore we may ask from our Lover
> to have all of him that we desire.
> For it is our nature to long for him,
> and it is his nature to long for us.

When two people are in love, they can't wait to converse. They can't wait to hear what the other has been doing all day; they want to know each other's hopes and dreams, thoughts and desires. If we are in love with God, we will want to hear his voice - we will long for it. The more we love God, the more we will want to grow quiet so we can hear him. It may take a while to catch on. Just as Samuel heard God call his name but didn't know it was God, we might have a few false starts. Our world is noisy with many distractions, and the most harmful distraction is the inclination to feel guilty about not doing our prayers "right." When you experience these disturbances, gently bring yourself back to listening; if your mind wanders or you fall asleep, so be it. The disciples themselves couldn't stay awake when Jesus was with them in the flesh! Jan Johnson recently wrote an article on prayer for *Conversations*, a journal about spiritual formation. She refers to different voices in the mind as committee members whose distracting messages play into our own unhealthy dynamics, causing us to feel guilty, overextend ourselves, feel superior about helping others, and so on. It is important to recognize these voices, name them, and then lay them aside, refocusing on what God is actually saying. Doing this helps us set aside negative associations with scriptural meditation and find freedom and relationship as we move toward interacting fully with the very life of God.

It is important to keep trying! Setting aside 15 minutes a day to be quiet in God's presence can lead to transformation and tremendous spiritual growth. It can also help us hear in our souls what God is doing when we find ourselves on the potter's wheel. Following are some exercises that have been helpful for people as they began to change the way they prayed. Doing these kinds of prayers regularly will move you from closed, controlled soliloquy to an open-ended, receptive posture.

PRAYING THE SCRIPTURE

For people whose minds wander (which is just about everyone) or who are depressed and have a hard time concentrating, praying the Scripture can help. Try the following exercise: Choose a verse or short passage that is particularly meaningful for you. For the sake of illustration, let's use the verse, "There is therefore now no condemnation for those who are in Christ Jesus" (Romans 8: 1). Say each word slowly and carefully. Ask the Holy Spirit to come and reveal the meaning these words have for you today, right now. Say them again, prayerfully, aware that God's presence surrounds you and that these are his utterances to you in love. Breathe deeply and let the words of the text fill you up inside. What would it mean if you really believed this – that there was no condemnation in Christ Jesus? How would you feel? How would you live? Close your eyes and open your palms in your lap. Pray the words, saying them again, realizing that they are true because they are God's words, and God does not lie. Allow the Holy Spirit to take you on from there, saying the words as often as you need or simply resting in God's love. If you journal, write down any insights that came to you during this time. If you do this with other people, share together after you are done.

This is a different way of reading Scripture than dissecting it—chopping it up to find everything we can about its historical content and garnering all the data possible. In a Conversations article Brian McLaren likens it to the two ways we can know a frog. We can dissect a frog and lay it open, learning all its parts as it lies there dead and cold. Or we can observe that frog living and active in its natural habitat, jumping from lily pad to bank to log. The latter is like praying the Scripture. It is a way to let the living words of God do what they do best as with disciplined passivity we let Scripture "read" us and allow it to bring about change.

GUIDED PRAYER

Sometimes guided prayer helps people create space in which to hear God's voice and receive his guidance. The following is an exercise in praying the Lord's Prayer (Matthew 6:9-13). Creating this kind of meditative prayerful attitude allows the Holy Spirit to at least slow down the hamster wheel for a time. Think about each part of the passage as you pray.

Our Father. This is a gracious address. Jesus doesn't keep his intimate relationship with God for himself but includes us all in it. Rest for a moment in the reality that Jesus' closeness with God is also something you are invited to participate in.

In heaven, hallowed be your name. God is other than us. Dwell in the assurance that Christ is the bridge from our brokenness to God's bright and beautiful reality.

Your kingdom come, your will be done, on earth as it is in heaven. Ask God for a few moments to make what's "up there" in heaven come "down here" in your life. Then ask him to create in you a longing for his kingdom to be established on earth at your workplace, in your family, with your friends. Pause and think about what this would look like for you.

Give us this day our daily bread. This is a call to trust. Relax for a moment in the truth that each day God will be enough for you and will provide for you. That's what he promised. Allow yourself the comfort of trusting him.

And forgive us our debts, as we also have forgiven our debtors. This is the only statement with a condition. Ask Jesus to help you love the world enough to let go of any grudges or resentments you have been holding. Ask him to forgive you for anything you need it for, and receive that forgiveness completely.

And do not bring us to the time of trial, but rescue us from the evil one. Fear is the enemy of the saints. Absorb the reality of the good shepherd leading you in safe places: keeping you, holding you, protecting you. When you are ready, open your eyes and reflect on any insights you received.

CENTERING PRAYER

I learned about centering prayer (even though I didn't know then what it was called) when we were attacked by a mother bear high above the timberline in the Adirondacks of New York. We were in our Sears pop-up tent, which was basically made of Saran Wrap. The baby bear had wandered into our campsite a few moments earlier and had been scared off by a backpack falling to the ground off a tree branch. When the mother came racing into our campsite, there was no ignoring her. She threw logs, ripped open zippers, tore backpacks, scattered dishware. Tim did what he had learned in the camping guide we had purchased at the ranger station-bang pots and pans together to scare off the bear. Guess what? It didn't work. She came charging at the tent, pushing her big flat head against the Saran Wrap wall that threatened to cave in on us, and she roared with horrible halitosis just inches from my face.

I was not feeling particularly spiritual at the moment. I could not pray I was shaking like a leaf lying there in my sleeping bag. Tim was scared too. After all, he was the one who had banged all those pots together! We waited with lumps the size of golf balls in our throats and heard our hearts pounding out what we thought to be the very last beats of our lives. But then these words came to my lips: "Lord Jesus Christ, have mercy on me." As I whispered them a peace flooded me that was from a Source outside myself. As the furious bear circled the tent I became calm. Finally, as I continued to whisper these words, she crashed off into the bushes and left.

Centering prayer helps at moments like these. Learning some simple phrases such as "Lord Jesus Christ, have mercy on me" or "Come, Lord Jesus" or "Be with me, 0 Lord; hold me in your steadfast love" can help us in times of crisis when we don't have a clue where to begin. When these words become internalized, the Holy Spirit prays them for you at moments when you cannot.

These phrases can be used also in our regular times of prayer. Breathing deeply, in and out, we can imagine ourselves breathing in the Holy Spirit and exhaling any tension or anxiety. We can ask for forgiveness, and then we can imagine ourselves opening our hands and releasing any resentment we are holding. As we do this we can pray our phrase again and again, perhaps visualizing a cross or another symbol of God's love. As we repeat the words over and over, cultivating an attitude of love and openness, we stay in a posture of receptivity and create space for Jesus to flood us with his presence.

Prayer is a conduit for the work of the Holy Spirit. It opens a channel through which we make ourselves available to God's healing touch. Whenever we surrender in prayer as has been described, even if we don't realize it, we have been shaped in some way by the potter's hand.

This shaping is not without purpose. Transformation not only changes us, but it changes others' experience of us! In the next chapter, we're going to consider the twelfth and final step of the 12 steps.

Chapter 16

A Spiritual Awakening

Teresa McBean

I have this friend, Joanne, who showed up in our little community all beaten up and battered by family suffering. I didn't know her well enough in those early days to realize the extent of her situation. It was clear on that first Sunday that she didn't want to be chatted up. She and her husband found obscure seating in the back row and hoped no one would notice them. In hindsight, this was a neon sign of desperation, because she and Craig are the warmest, friendliest couple you'd ever want to meet. Many of us show up at Northstar Community because of addiction or other plaguing, relentless, hamster wheel sufferings. Joanne and Craig soon realized that they fit right in, and they felt safe to come clean, join community, and find loving relationships. In the years since, Joanne and Craig have ministered to other newcomers who have had similar life struggles. It seemed like their hamster wheel suffering was being used for a purpose (and it was!).

But this week, God has revealed more of his plan. A young person in our community has received a diagnosis of a particularly ugly form of cancer. This is completely shocking, and we're all reeling from such unexpected news. Joanne, it turns out, has years of experience as an oncology nurse. Who better to send to the bedside of a freaking out family than…Joanne? And guess what? These two families were friends, united in a different, more typical kind of community suffering.

Late in the evening, after a particularly grueling day of chemotherapy, Joanne called me and said, "You know, all these years I thought God was using me in a certain way, but it turns out, that I think all those years ago, God knew there would be this day. And on this day, all those past years of relationship, and my calling as a nurse, they come together so that I can be of service to this particular family." I love this story. If Joanne and Craig hadn't been willing to hop on the wheel and stay there long past the suffering that brought them to their knees, we wouldn't have had such capable hands in which to entrust this family. The rest of us can do the meal thing. Scott, our Associate Pastor and I, can do the pastoral thing. But no one else can offer what Joanne is offering.

NIMBLE SPIRITUALITY

Thanks be to God for spiritual awakenings.

> Step 12: Having had a spiritual awakening, we tried to carry this message to others and to practice these principles in all our affairs.

"I just can't look at myself in the mirror anymore."

"I am not the person I thought I would be when I grew up."

"This isn't who I really am."

"Have you ever woken up in the morning, seen your reflection in the mirror, and not known who that person is staring back at you?"

"I am so ashamed."

"I don't know what has happened to me; I've lost myself. I'm a stranger to myself."

I hear these sentiments expressed by hurting people on a regular basis—heck, I feel this disconnect between the person I am today and the person I dream of becoming. This "waking up" is a glorious, sacred, and sometimes secret truth, and the journey is uneven, filled with backtracks and rabbit trails. Finding our way back to God isn't a quick fix or a magic pill, but it can be an awesome life.

A passage of scripture that reminds me of my life's work is found in the book of Ephesians.

> It's in Christ that we find out who we are and what we are living for. Long before we first heard of Christ and got our hopes up, he had his eye on us, had designs on us for glorious living, part of the overall purpose he is working out in everything and everyone. It's in Christ that you, once you heard the truth and believed it (this Message of your salvation), found yourselves home free—signed, sealed, and delivered by the Holy Spirit. This signet from God is the first installment on what's coming, a reminder that we'll get everything God has planned for us, a praising and glorious life. (Ephesians 1:11-14 The Message)

This praising and glorious life—this God who is in the business of working this purpose out in everything and everyone—is ours for the living. We can bring the message of hope to hurting people once we've lived it. Take a moment to prayerfully reflect. Once ashamed, without hope, and certainly helpless, we may have lost some things along the way that were important to us. We lost ourselves. Who we once were is gone, and a new creation lives. Once upon a time, we lost our confidence and our belief in ourselves and in God.

Sometimes I need a reminder of the possibilities that await me if I will surrender myself to God's care and control. When I get discouraged, I have a notebook with suggestions about how I have worked through this malaise in the past. Selections from Proverbs can also provide quick reminders of what the future holds for someone willing to do the work of recovery. For example:

Hear, for I will speak excellent and princely things; and the opening of my lips shall be for right things. For my mouth shall utter truth, and wrongdoing is detestable and loathsome to my lips. All the words of my mouth are righteous (upright and in right standing with God; one whose aim is true); there is nothing contrary to truth or crooked in them. (Proverbs 8:6-8 AMP)

Sometimes we fall down, but there is beauty in recognizing that both the fall and the return from disgrace are beautiful parts of our story. May God richly bless as we continue on this journey of faith. On those occasions when we notice that our performance isn't matching our potential, remember who it is that works in and through us—it never was about the performance. Remember the process of humbling self and hunting for God that led us to this point. As those who have gone before us, we fight the good fight. As we are responsible to God, he will never disappoint.

A spiritual awakening is part of effective 12-step work and a hallmark of the potter's wheel lifestyle. I find that people who have spiritual awakenings possess the ability to see the world through what I like to call "God-vision goggles." Some people have dramatic moments of clarity. Others experience it as a process. Many say that it was in hindsight that they became aware of God's hand on their lives. My friend, Joanne, for example, thought she had clarity of viewpoint until this recent event with our family in medical crisis. Today she realizes that she has only seen, as the scriptures say, "in part, as through a mirror darkly."

For years, evangelicals have used the term "born again." Although many scorn this phrase, I think it clearly describes what happens—an awakening in our hearts to God. My spiritually awake friends all agree that it's an "a-ha" experience. It's hard to describe if you've never experienced it for yourself. (Read 1 Corinthians 2 for a better understanding as to why this is a tough concept to describe.)

Scripture talks about this process in the book of 2 Corinthians:

> Praise be to the God and Father of our Lord Jesus Christ, the Father of compassion and the God of all comfort, who comforts us in all our troubles, so that we can comfort those in

any trouble with the comfort we ourselves have received from God. (2 Corinthians 1:3-4 NIV)

This is God's plan for ministry. It works like this. As we grow up in our spirituality, we begin to see ourselves more accurately and develop the discernment to see others with clarity of vision too. As we move through the growing up process, we develop life experience, which teaches us about compassion and empathy. Sometimes, by the grace of God, we meet people who are ready for potter's wheel living. When this happens, it is a God thing.

Frankly, many people lose hope in solutions. They believe the lie that nothing will ever change. When scripture says that we are ambassadors for Christ, this is what that verse means. We have been sent to use our experience, strength, and hope to carry this good news to other hurting people. Often God puts people in our path with the exact same hurt that we have experienced. In Genesis (50:20), Joseph speaks of this miraculous working of God. He's been seriously mistreated in his life, but he learned through his own spiritual awakening how to rise above the obstacles and turn them into opportunities. When confronted by his former tormentors (his brothers), Joseph says this: "You intended to harm me, but God intended it for good to accomplish what is now being done, the saving of many lives." God is the ultimate recycler. He takes our pain and powerfully moves in and through us to bring good out of situations that are thoroughly evil. This process is thwarted if we haven't worked through our own pain. Richard Rohr says that if we don't learn how to transform our pain, we'll continue to transmit it. This is hamster-wheel living. When we've begun to live out the solution, rather than wallow in the problem, we might find that we have changed—and the process may feel quite mysterious.

Here are some principles that I've learned from scripture that help me live out my own life on the potter's wheel:

a) It is God who makes us both willing and able to fulfill his good purpose. (See Philippians 2:13 and 2 Corinthians 1:20-22).

b) We serve a God who is able and willing to transform us. God's plans cannot be thwarted. ("My purpose will stand, and I will do all that I please." See Isaiah 46:9-11.)

c) We've been given one instruction: to believe. When we take responsibility to believe, God assumes responsibility for the outcome. I can only assume that God is a big enough God to handle my predisposed shortcomings and defects of character. (Study John 6:29; Exodus 14:14; 2 Chronicles 16:9)

d) God has said he will equip us. Who am I to doubt? (Read 2 Timothy 3:16-17)

In our humanity, all these plans are not immediately obvious to us. We are easily deceived and distracted, and we regularly deny the truth about our lives. Our work will require that we actively seek to live out in the open, with nothing hidden. Listen to how the Apostle Paul talks about this process:

Whenever anyone turns to the Lord, the veil is taken away. Now the Lord is the Spirit, and where the Spirit of the Lord is, there is freedom. And we, who with unveiled faces all reflect the Lord's glory, are being transformed into his likeness with ever-increasing glory, which comes from the Lord, who is the Spirit. 2 Corinthians 3:16-18 (NIV)

Recently I had cataracts removed, and let me tell you, there is a lot of cool stuff to see in this world. I see clearly and in full color for the first time in a long time, and it's awesome! We find the Lord in the unseen world. It is there that we meet God, and it is there that we find freedom. You were created to be free. This freedom cannot be bought, bartered, or begged for—only God provides freedom.

As Paul says, when we meet the Spirit of the Lord and find our freedom, we become a reflection of God's glory. This is a process; the transformation takes place in "ever-increasing glory." This glory is a bestowed glory, merely a reflection of the Lord's glory—a truth so profound that it eliminates any hint of arrogance or pride. It is a humbling glory, but glory indeed—a shining that draws others to us. We are now ready to carry God's message of hope to hurting people. This is that "new place" that Kim is going to talk about in the next chapter.

Chapter 17

Finding Ourselves in a New Place

Kim Engelmann

All that I have said up to this point is for one purpose only—to free the people of God so they can live triumphantly as the church Jesus died to save. That is why I have shared my own story so openly—that I might prove redemptive for you. If a traumatic event has occurred in your life, whether a recent incident in an ongoing cycle or something that's happened for the first time, it doesn't have to keep you in bondage. Here is a summary of the process of transition from hamster wheel to potter's wheel.

State the problem. It is common to deny the significance of trauma, to minimize the issue and therefore not take steps to get help. So the first step is to admit there is a problem. We may need help, a decent community with experience in both suffering and healing, to help us unmask our past attempts to avoid naming our problems accurately. We will need to assess whether or not we have used superficial spiritual language to hide behind and avoid the pervasive underlying issues that need to be articulated and addressed. We may need to evaluate our current practices of worship. Have we avoided the church, or are we attending a church that is unhelpful in our recovery process? I wish every church had the skills necessary to help us walk through this "problem naming" process, but if we don't currently have that resource, we need to look for it. Churches with recovery ministries, vibrant care ministries, counseling centers and such may have resources that some churches simply cannot provide. If the problem involves violence, depression or other mental illness, addiction, depletion or an ongoing repetitive pattern, chances are talking about it within our family system won't do the trick. Under these conditions, even if we can articulate the problem, we will need some kind of outside assistance to help us work it through. No one can put out a fire from inside the building that is collapsing on them. (Notice that we're saying the old structures of our lives–family, friends, church–may need to be evaluated for effectiveness in finding a solution to our problem. This is not casting judgment, it is saying that we need to take responsibility for finding resources that can help us with transformative recovery.)

Reach out. Maybe we don't know what our problem is, but we realize that we are being dragged down and feeling hopeless most of the time. We may need, as stated above, outside expertise to help us discover our issue. I pray that each of us can summon up our courage and accept responsibility for reaching out for help. If our first "asks" don't result in finding what we need, we may need to keep asking. This needs to be safe help – and we may even need help figuring out who to ask for help! Don't give up–there are people who can help us.

Begin to seek God in some of the "open-ended" ways we talked about in our chapters on prayer. For further learning in this area, there are numerous books and resources available. Ongoing prayer support from people who know how to pray is another option. Form a prayer chain or find one where people can receive prayer every day on a consistent basis. In our prayer chain ministry, the person being prayed for will "check in" bi-weekly, which helps the pray-ers know what is happening, how to pray and when to rejoice.

Involve others in your journey. As I have emphasized repeatedly, our wounds are not meant to stay hidden forever. We may not want to just spill our guts anywhere or to just anyone, and this is appropriate. Good boundaries are necessary. At the same time, as we grow and heal, involving others in our journey toward health and wholeness will help us realize that we are not alone. As we open up one to another, we indirectly give others permission to share as well.

Look for opportunities. As we begin to feel stronger, we can ask where God is calling us to serve. (This is known as the twelfth step in recovery communities.) Where can our wounds be used redemptively? How can we bring the opportunity to experience freedom and healing to others? As we explore possibilities, it may well be that our healing will be enhanced through giving. A cautionary note: The timing here is very important. The last thing we want to do is to give before we have learned to receive OR to give in order to avoid the pain of potter's-wheel transformation. We can share our ideas for service with people who have walked with us through our pain to see what they think about our service ideas, which provides us needed feedback and prayer support.

There is nothing easy about working our way from hamster wheel to potter's wheel living. It was difficult for my husband and me to get help and get healed—we didn't change wheels in a flying leap. Little by little we dealt with our problems, addressing them gradually in therapy and recovery community, making a conscious effort to change old patterns.

Tim and I went out to dinner recently and had a marvelous time at our favorite restaurant. Out of the blue, he turned and looked at me.

"Thanks so much for taking me back into your life," he said.

"I love you," I replied.

"It wasn't easy," he said, looking at me with steady hazel eyes. "It was a tremendous risk."

"That's what you do when you love someone. You risk. You are worth taking back."

Then I cried. I cried because it had all worked out so darn well, despite all the doomsday predictions and heartache. We had gone somewhere together! It had been a potter's-wheel process. I sat not long ago with a man from another church who had given his life to the ministry and whose wife had been unfaithful. It had been a terrible ordeal. The couple was well known. The scandal had rocked the congregation and the community in many ways. This man was going through a period of seeking the Lord and trying to figure out how to get on with his life. It was tremendously difficult for him. On top of it all, a close family member died during this same period. After talking with him at length, I shared that I was writing a book and that I was trying to make some distinctions between hamster-wheel versus potter's-wheel suffering.

"What do you think?" I asked him. "Is there something that you would point to that would distinguish the two?"

"Yes," he said. "Despite all of this pain and difficulty, the betrayal and the shame, there are moments of joy that keep invading my life. Jesus is with me in this, and that is sustaining me. To have joy spurt up in the midst of all this is ridiculous. And yet I keep being refreshed. I know that I am not alone."

It is hard to work our way toward emotional freedom, just as it is hard for any slave to leave bondage. It was difficult for the Southern slaves to travel North toward freedom. It was hard for the Israelites to escape from Egypt; it took courage to cross the Red Sea (even with Moses and his miraculous sea-parting powers). How stressful was it for the Jews to make the decision to flee Nazi Germany? What about the Jews who endured concentration camp living? When we read or watch accounts of terrible conditions of bondage and torture for so many people, don't we want for them to find freedom?

In the movie *The Shawshank Redemption*, Andy, the main character, is imprisoned for murdering his wife–a crime he didn't commit. The warden of the prison is corrupt, and he kills the one witness who could set Andy free. So over the years, Andy slowly chisels a tunnel through his cell wall, hidden by a large poster of Rita Hayworth. One night Andy crawls through the tunnel, swims through a putrid sewer and ends up outside the maximum security prison that held him captive for so many years.

"He's free!" you want to yell. "Yes! He made it! Run Andy, run!" Andy does make it to freedom and begins a new life, but not until he brings about the downfall of the evil warden. The delight this story evokes is exhilarating.

I think that when we do an about-face on the things that keep us in bondage, God is delighted. As Jesus tells us, "There will be more joy in heaven over one sinner who repents than over ninety-nine righteous persons who need no repentance." (Luke 15:7).

Sin means "missing the mark". Imagine an arrow shot from a bow that goes wide of its target. We miss the mark when we live shackled to the hamster wheel. We miss the mark when we make someone other than God our god. We miss the mark when we believe in a god who is not God. We miss the mark when we decide there is no way of escape. But when we are liberated, there is rejoicing in heaven (and in communities who understand this fierce battle for the spiritual warfare that it is, there is rejoicing on earth too).

"Yes!" the heavenly hosts cry. "You've made it out. You've discovered the glorious liberty of the children of God!" A party is thrown; a banquet is held in your honor. That's more than a Shawshank redemption, that's an eternal redemption.

I meet people who are trying hard to be good people, and yet they're caught in a destructive cycle of unproductive suffering. Christians slog on, believing that they are on mission to "do God's will," but having no idea that God's will is precisely not what they're doing. Too harsh? Think about my mother's words. Certainly that kind of verbal abuse and God-slander fits in this category (Deuteronomy 6 gives us a different perspective on parenting).

I am reminded of Kierkegaard's parable of the duck pastor who preached every Sunday to all the town's ducks at the church in the square. One day the duck pastor discovered that all ducks had wings and possessed the ability to fly. He couldn't wait until Sunday morning for his "flock" to arrive at church.

"You know," he told them, "We can fly! We can soar! We are not land-bound. We can circle the skies!"

The ducks in the congregation were impressed. "Great sermon!" they told the duck pastor. And then they all walked home.

If we believe the gospel, we can forget over time how wonderful the good news is–especially if we cannot figure out how to live the good news on a daily basis. I remember starting a class I was teaching with a summation of the gospel message.

"Jesus died so that you could have a close, intimate relationship with God and live the abundant life right here on earth and forever in heaven with him. You are forgiven and you don't have to fear death anymore," I said.

Someone yawned.

Someone else looked forlornly at the snack table where the last piece of cake had just been taken.

Others picked at their nails.

This was a class of "saints" who regularly teach – some of the most active, stalwart members of our church.

"So," I said. "Why aren't you more excited?"

There was a moment's pause. Then they chuckled, then they laughed and finally they started clapping. They had heard it so many times they were used to this wonderful news. For those who have been in church all our lives, we can suffer from long-term believers' glaze–a kind of spiritual hypnosis that hits us whenever we hear the standard gospel message, like John 3:16, or other familiar truths. Maybe we are grace-fatigued. If we practice the twelve steps, especially those pesky middle ones–where we name our shortcomings to God, self and another human–our complacency over this good news is tantamount to denial of the highest order.

Our spiritual sleepiness, our stubborn resistance to surrender, our unwillingness to see ourselves accurately, our need to judge others and withhold love–these truths can pull the rug of fake-normalcy out from under us, and invite us into a life of risky love, lived in hope and outrageous trust. We'll show up for celebrations and parties–because we cannot forget the standing ovation our own experience that practicing faith elicits.

We cannot stay on the hamster-wheel when we are telling ourselves the truth about our condition. However, if we find a way to practice what we believe, we discover compassion and empathy for others. This, indeed, is an exciting life.

"But I don't know what God's will is for me," a young woman sobbed after I suggested the above. "It's all very nice what you say," she continued, dabbing tears with a tissue. "But I pray and I pray and I just don't know what to do."

Every so often God gives us Cliffs Notes in Scripture–little summations so that if we haven't gotten the truth by doing the "Bible in One Year" regimen, we can still get it. Jesus' *Bible for Dummies* says, "Look, the whole law and the prophets is summed up in the following: "Love the Lord your god with all you heart, soul and mind and your neighbor as yourself." (Luke 10:27). A quick and dirty version for the confused, time-constrained Bible reading dropout. God also sums it up for us in Micah 6:8: "And what does the Lord require of you but to do justice, and to love kindness, and to walk humbly with your God?"

When confused, we can take these summations of Scripture to heart. Knowing that we cannot please everyone and that we already please God, because he loves us, we can ask, "What does the Lord require of me?" This question, when asked as part of our potter's-wheel lifestyle, is motivated from a place of gratitude. Tim, my husband, and I know our lives could have turned out differently! We are so .....grateful. It's like saying, "What's next, Papa?" We don't have to try to live up to a standard of "goodness" in order to receive God's love or avoid his disapproval. My goodness! If God never does another single thing for us, the restoration of our family is more than enough to leave us breathlessly grateful and eager to express it in our daily living.

To do justice. Justice is more than fairness. Fairness tries to make external circumstances equal, but justice isn't based on external appearance. Justice values people, circumstances, motivation and context. It takes into account the entire picture. God is a God of justice, and we cannot further the cause of justice for others if we have not pursued it for ourselves. In recovery rooms, attenders often hear that we cannot give away that which we do not possess, understand, and experience. Staying stuck on the hamster-wheel, refusing to name the problem and take responsibility for participating in the solution–that does not perpetuate justice. It creates a downward spiral into hamster-wheel frenzy. God doesn't value the external; God looks beyond and sees the whole picture completely. Are you in need of God's justice? Pursue it!

To love mercy. Mercy wants to create a world full of merciful people, not perpetuate violence and oppression. Mercy is not feeling sorry for people; it is doing what will most help them become whole. Sometimes this is tricky as we navigate the complexity of enabling versus helping. Are we keeping an unmerciful situation going by giving in and not rocking the boat? Or are we assisting in someone's opportunity to experience recovery? We ask this of ourselves as well. Is our lack of initiative in getting out of the hamster wheel actually intensifying unmerciful conditions? Do we need mercy? Act on this inclination.

To walk humbly with your God. Humility is only true humility when it comes out of a sense of our own worth in God's eyes. Passivity is not humility; fear is not humility; groveling is not humility. Humility springs from a deep knowledge that we are loved and held secure. We don't have to prove anything anymore. We have One on our side who is utterly reliable, utterly faithful, utterly for us. This gives us courage to move forward and walk with God in dependence and trust, to move to the rhythms of justice, love and mercy that set us free. This entire study is an invitation to live in the joyful reality of this empowering dependence.

Epilogue

Teresa McBean and Kim Engelmann

When Kim and I began the project of updating her book *Running In Circles*, we had no idea that it would morph into the scope that we ended up tackling. I feel like a woman who has walked into another woman's kitchen and rearranged her cabinets! Kim trusted me to nip and tuck, insert here and there, and I really appreciate her trust. I'm not sure how you will experience this melding of two worlds—hers church, I think, and mine more recovery—both distinctly Christian. It is our prayer that we've somehow managed to communicate the truth of our journeys within the context of our respective communities in such a way that no matter your perspective, we will somehow connect. This, we believe, is the work of the Holy Spirit, and even now we pray that it might be alive and active among us.

One small closing story before I turn you back to Kim for her personal epilogue.

We had talked about this project several times over the phone, East Coast to West. We managed to figure out the time changes (don't laugh, this is hard for us) and between our busy schedules, we chatted. For me, talking to Kim is like experiencing streams of living waters rushing through my soul.

Anyway, I happened to be in California on vacation and my husband was going to hang out at the Masters and watch a little golf (torturous for me), and I thought, hey, Kim is in California, I'll email her and see if she has time to talk while I'm in the same time zone! Long story short, when we caught up, she could practically see the roof of the hotel I was staying in from her home. We had a lovely lunch together, which was unforgettable for me.

Imagine if I hadn't called. I'd have never known she was so close, we would have never taken time to sit outside in the sun and dine finely. I think this is how it is with us and God. We forget how close he is; we cannot imagine that he would take time to eat a crab salad with us in the sun. If you've never known this, if you've never experienced this closeness – oh please, listen to Kim's story and soak up the suggestions she makes. Get a small group of friends together and work the workbook within community. For those of you who have done this, I applaud you! Let us hear from you – we're always looking for a good excuse to grab lunch with a new friend!

Now, here's Kim:

It took me a while to decide to share my story. I hesitated because I was worried about what people would think of me. Then one day I decided I didn't care. I realized that if I shirked from telling it, I was negating the power of God that had kept me sane and alive during years of insanity. At first I shared with trembling, but gradually it became easier. I am convinced that it is the most helpful thing I have to offer people, and in a very real sense it is all I have to offer. What is more convincing to people of Christ's love and power than our own stories of his faithfulness? How do we prove the resurrection to Thomas? By showing our wounds John 20:26-28).

People ask me about my mother, and I have to tell them that I really don't know much about her anymore. She is still alive, but for the safety of my children and my own stability, I have made the choice not to have contact with her. I have been honest and told her she needs help, but I don't think she will ever accept this. Do I pray for her? Yes. Have I forgiven her? Absolutely—although it took a while. One day I came upon a definition of resentment that startled me. Resentment, according to this definition, was feeling the same thing over and over. In my case, a negative, hardened and judgmental attitude toward my mother kept cycling through my life, like circling planes with nowhere to land. These circling planes of negative emotion were draining my energy and focus. Gradually I have let those planes come down through forgiveness.

The harder person to forgive was my father, but I have worked my way through that one as well. He was intelligent, creative and entertaining—trained at Menninger, a bastion of charm, genius and wit. I don't know why he couldn't seem to get my mother the help she needed, but for whatever reason it was beyond him. He helped many people to know Jesus, and what he provided in love gave me just enough fiber to survive. He wasn't always there, but he was there enough.

Anne Lamott has said in *Bird by Bird* that resentment is like drinking rat poison and waiting for the rat to die. That is not how I want to spend the rest of my days. I want to live, really live, in joy and not let life pass me by. As my therapy continues to unfold, as my prayer life deepens, as my trust in God increases, I find myself noticing things I have never noticed before. I am more amazed and full of wonder at the richness of life each year, like a kid gawking at a banana split for the first time - the ripples of whipped topping, the different colors of ice cream, the swirling fudge sliding off the side.

Yes, the rich texture of life amazes me. I look at my children and can scarcely believe the miracle that they are, growing up beautiful, healthy, competent and, inevitably, much taller than me. I love to ocean kayak with them and Tim, and I marvel at the expansive Pacific. I appreciate it like a gift - the gulls calling, the loons dipping and the sea lion popping above the surface of the water to stare at me with bright black eyes. It is as if I am finally alive, feeling, breathing, taking in grace.

One day I went to look at the yard I used to play in as a child. Of course it had shrunk beyond belief. The tree I had climbed was much shorter, and a branch I used to sit on had been sawed off. The wooden fence was still there, dark and moist from a recent rain, and on one end webs of leafless ivy sprawled up the side. Dirty snow and mud surrounded the bottom of the fence posts.

I remembered how daunting that fence had seemed to me—high and severe with no places to peek through. Now I could easily look over the top and see a child playing basketball in the neighbor's driveway and the newly remodeled playground across the street. The yard was flat where I had played out so much of my young life. That small square of patchy lawn and stained snow had been my entire world for a long time.

I think about Jesus. He came from a wide expansive place to our meager plot of stained soil called Earth. When he came he pointed beyond our fences, beyond the flatness of life. He tried to show us that if we would just have the courage to listen and trust, life expands in all glorious directions. If we allowed him he would lift us up and over to expelience the glorious liberty of the children of God.

We hold in tension the reality of our current condition and the already/not-yet promise that "death will be no more; mourning and crying and pain will be no more" (Revelation 21:4). We catch glimpses of the fulfillment of this promise now during our earthly journey-healings, conversions, new inspirations, being aware of God's presence. We see in a glass dimly, but one day we shall see face to face.

For Additional
Recovery Resources
visit
www.nacr.org

The National Association
for Christian Recovery

Made in the USA
Charleston, SC
10 March 2014